CAMBRIDGE LIBRARY COLLECTION

Books of enduring scholarly value

History

The books reissued in this series include accounts of historical events and movements by eye-witnesses and contemporaries, as well as landmark studies that assembled significant source materials or developed new historiographical methods. The series includes work in social, political and military history on a wide range of periods and regions, giving modern scholars ready access to influential publications of the past.

On the Education of the People of India

Charles Edward Trevelyan (1807–1886) published *Education of the People of India* in 1838. The work is a rigorous defence of the educational reforms that took place in colonial India during the 1830s, which led to a western-based curriculum replacing traditional Indian learning. The work is a response to the arguments of orientalists such as H. H. Wilson (1786–1860), recently retired from government office in India, but still advocating an orientalist educational policy. In this work Trevelyan puts forward his arguments for the moral and intellectual advantages of English as the principle language of instruction and defends the government's resolution of March 1835 that specified that Indians should be educated by the study of European literature, culture and science. It was one of the most influential Anglicist tracts of the Indian educational debates, and it gives valuable insight into the ideas behind what became standard government educational policy.

Cambridge University Press has long been a pioneer in the reissuing of out-of-print titles from its own backlist, producing digital reprints of books that are still sought after by scholars and students but could not be reprinted economically using traditional technology. The Cambridge Library Collection extends this activity to a wider range of books which are still of importance to researchers and professionals, either for the source material they contain, or as landmarks in the history of their academic discipline.

Drawing from the world-renowned collections in the Cambridge University Library, and guided by the advice of experts in each subject area, Cambridge University Press is using state-of-the-art scanning machines in its own Printing House to capture the content of each book selected for inclusion. The files are processed to give a consistently clear, crisp image, and the books finished to the high quality standard for which the Press is recognised around the world. The latest print-on-demand technology ensures that the books will remain available indefinitely, and that orders for single or multiple copies can quickly be supplied.

The Cambridge Library Collection will bring back to life books of enduring scholarly value (including out-of-copyright works originally issued by other publishers) across a wide range of disciplines in the humanities and social sciences and in science and technology.

On the Education of the People of India

CHARLES EDWARD TREVELYAN

CAMBRIDGE UNIVERSITY PRESS

Cambridge, New York, Melbourne, Madrid, Cape Town,
Singapore, São Paolo, Delhi, Tokyo, Mexico City

Published in the United States of America by Cambridge University Press, New York

www.cambridge.org
Information on this title: www.cambridge.org/9781108276641

This edition first published 1838
This digitally printed version 2011

ISBN 978-1-108-27664-1 Paperback

ON

THE EDUCATION

OF THE

PEOPLE OF INDIA.

ON

THE EDUCATION

OF

THE PEOPLE OF INDIA.

BY

CHARLES E. TREVELYAN, ESQ.

OF THE BENGAL CIVIL SERVICE.

LONDON:

LONGMAN, ORME, BROWN, GREEN, & LONGMANS,

PATERNOSTER-ROW.

1838.

CONTENTS

CHAPTER I.

CHAPTER II.

THE EDUCATION

THE PEOPLE OF INDIA.

CHAPTER I.

*The Measures first adopted for educating the Natives.—
The Establishment of the Committee of Public In-
struction. — Their first Plan of Operations. — The
Difference of Opinion which arose.—The Resolution
of Government of the 7th March 1835. — The Mea-
sures adopted by the Committee in consequence. —
No Distinction of Caste allowed in the new Semi-
naries. — Cultivation of the vernacular Languages.
— Education of the Wards of Government. — The
Medical College. — Mr. Adam's Deputation.*

THE history of the first efforts made by us for the
education of our Indian fellow-subjects may be
told in a few words. The Mohammedan college
at Calcutta was established A.D. 1781, and the
Sanskrit college at Benares A.D. 1792. The

B

course of study at these institutions was purely oriental, and the object of it was to provide a regular supply of qualified Hindu and Mohammedan law officers for the judicial administration. The next step taken was at the renewal of the Company's charter in 1813, when 10,000*l.*, or a lac of rupees a year, was set apart "for the revival and promotion of literature, and the encouragement of the learned natives of India, and for the introduction and promotion of a knowledge of the sciences among the inhabitants of the British territories." The subject was however regarded at that time in India with so much apathy, that no measures were adopted to fulfil the intentions of the British legislature till 1823. On the 17th of July in that year the governor general in council resolved, that "there should be constituted a general committee of public instruction for the purpose of ascertaining the state of public education, and of the public institutions designed for its promotion, and of considering, and from time to time submitting to government, the suggestion of such measures as it may appear expedient to adopt with a view to the better instruction of the people, to the introduction among them of useful knowledge, and to the improvement of their moral character." Corresponding instructions were addressed to the

gentlemen who were to compose the committee *,
and the arrears of the annual lac of rupees were
accounted for to them from the 1st May 1821.
From this period the general committee of public
instruction must be regarded as the sole organ of
the government in every thing that concerns that
important branch of its functions.

The first measures of the new committee were
to complete the organization of a Sanskrit college, then lately established by the government at
Calcutta, in lieu of two similar institutions, the
formation of which had been previously contemplated at Nuddea and Tirhoot; to take under their
patronage and greatly to improve the Hindu
college at Calcutta, which had been founded as
far back as 1816, by the voluntary contributions
of the natives themselves, for the instruction of
their youth in English literature and science; to
found two entirely new colleges at Delhi and Agra
for the cultivation of oriental literature; to commence the printing of Sanskrit and Arabic books

---

* In the instructions addressed to the committee, the object of
their appointment was stated to be the " considering and from time
to time submitting to government the suggestion of such measures
as it may appear expedient to adopt with a view to the better
instruction of the people, to the introduction of useful knowledge,
including the sciences and arts of Europe, and to the improvement
of their moral character."

on a great scale, besides liberally encouraging such undertakings by others; and to employ an accomplished oriental scholar in translating European scientific works into Arabic, upon which undertaking large sums were subsequently expended. English classes were afterwards established in connection with the Mohammedan and Sanskrit college at Calcutta, the Sanskrit college at Benares, and the Agra college; and a separate institution was founded at Delhi in 1829 for the cultivation of western learning, in compliance with the urgent solicitation of the authorities at that place.

The principles which guided the proceedings of the committee throughout this period are explained in the following extract from their printed report, dated in December 1831 : —

" The introduction of useful knowledge is the great object which they have proposed as the end of the measures adopted or recommended by them, keeping in view the necessity of consulting the feelings and conciliating the confidence of those for whose advantage their measures are designed.

" The committee has therefore continued to encourage the acquirement of the native literature of both Mohammedans and Hindus, in the institutions which they found established for these purposes, as the Madressa of Calcutta and Sanskrit college of Benares. They have also endeavoured to promote the activity of similar establishments, of which local considerations dictated the formation, as the Sanskrit college of Calcutta and the colleges of Agra and Delhi, as it is to such alone, even in the present day, that the influential and learned classes, those who are by birthright or profession teachers and expounders of literature, law, and religion, maulavis and pundits, willingly resort.

" In the absence of their natural patrons, the rich and powerful of their own creeds, the committee have felt it incumbent upon them to contribute to the support of the learned classes of India by literary endowments, which provide not only directly for a certain number, but indirectly for many more, who derive from collegiate acquirements consideration and subsistence amongst their countrymen. As far also as Mohammedan and Hindu law are concerned, an avenue is thus opened for them to public employment, and the state is provided with a supply of able servants and valuable subjects ; for there is no doubt that, imperfect as oriental learning may be in many respects, yet the higher the degree of the attainments even in it possessed by any native, the more intelligent and liberal he will prove, and the better qualified to appreciate the acts and designs of the government.

" But whilst every reasonable encouragement is given to indigenous native education, no opportunity has been omitted by the committee of improving its quality and adding to its value. In all the colleges the superintendence is European, and this circumstance is of itself an evidence and a cause of very important amelioration. In the Madressa of Calcutta and Hindu college of Benares, institutions of earlier days, European superintendence was for many years strenuously and successfully resisted. This opposition has long ceased. The consequences are a systematic course of study, diligent and regular habits, and an impartial appreciation of merits, which no institution left to native superintendence alone has ever been known to maintain.

" The plan of study adopted in the colleges is in general an improvement upon the native mode, and is intended to convey a well-founded knowledge of the languages studied, with a wider range of acquirement than is common, and to effect this in the least possible time. Agreeably to the native mode of instruction, for instance, a Hindu or Mohammedan lawyer devotes the best years of his life to the acquirement of law alone, and is very imperfectly acquainted with the language which treats of the subject of his studies. In the Madressa and Sanskrit college the first part of the course is now calculated to form a really good Arabic and Sanskrit scholar, and a competent knowledge of law is then acquired with comparative facility and contemporaneously with other branches of Hindu or Mohammedan learning.

" Again, the improvements effected have not been limited to a reformation in the course and scope of native study, but, whenever opportunity has favoured, new and better instruction has been grafted upon the original plan. Thus in the Madressa, Euclid has been long studied and with considerable advantage: European anatomy has also been introduced. In the Sanskrit college of Calcutta, European anatomy and medicine have nearly supplanted the native systems. At Agra and at Delhi the elements of geography and astronomy and mathematics are also part of the college course. To the Madressa, the Sanskrit college of Calcutta, and the Agra college, also, English classes are attached, whilst at Delhi and Benares distinct schools have been formed for the dissemination of the English language. Without offering therefore any violence to native prejudices, and whilst giving liberal encouragement to purely native education, the principle of connecting it with the introduction of real knowledge has never been lost sight of, and the foundation has been laid of great and beneficial change in the minds of those who by their character and profession direct and influence the intellect of Hindustan.

" In addition to the measures adopted for the diffusion of English in the provinces, and which are yet only in their infancy, the encouragement of the Vidyalaya, or Hindu college of Calcutta, has always been one of the chief objects of the committee's attention. The consequence has surpassed expectation. A command of the English language and a familiarity with its literature and science have been acquired to an extent rarely equalled by any schools in Europe. A taste for English has been widely disseminated, and independent schools, conducted by young men reared in the Vidyalaya, are springing up in every direction. The moral effect has been equally remarkable, and an impatience of the restrictions of Hinduism and a disregard of its ceremonies are openly avowed by many young men of respectable birth and talents, and entertained by many more who outwardly conform to the practices of their countrymen. Another generation will probably

witness a very material alteration in the notions
and feelings of the educated classes of the Hindu
community of Calcutta."

Meanwhile the progress of events was leading
to the necessity of adopting a more decided course.
The taste for English became more and more
" widely disseminated." A loud call arose for the
means of instruction in it, and the subject was
pressed on the committee from various quarters.
English books only were in any demand: upwards of thirty-one thousand English books were
sold by the school-book society in the course
of two years, while the education committee
did not dispose of Arabic and Sanskrit volumes
enough in three years to pay the expense of
keeping them for two months*, to say nothing
of the printing expenses. Among other signs of
the times, a petition was presented to the committee by a number of young men who had been
brought up at the Sanskrit college, pathetically
representing that, notwithstanding the long and

---

* The committee's book depository cost 638 rupees a month, or
about 765*l*. 12*s*. a year, of which 300*l*. a year was the salary of the
European superintendent. The sum realized by the sale of the
books during the three last years of the establishment was less than
100*l*. On the change of the committee's operations the whole of
this expense was saved, some of the books being transferred to the
Asiatic Society, and the rest placed under the charge of the secretary to the committee.

elaborate course of study which they had gone through, they had little prospect of bettering their condition; that the indifference with which they were generally regarded by their countrymen left them no hope of assistance from them, and that they therefore trusted that the government, which had made them what they were, would not abandon them to destitution and neglect. The English, classes which had been tacked on to this and other oriental colleges had entirely failed in their object. The boys had not time to go through an English, in addition to an oriental course, and the study which was secondary was naturally neglected. The translations into Arabic, also, appeared to have made as little impression upon the few who knew that language, as upon the mass of the people who were entirely unacquainted with it.

Under these circumstances a difference of opinion arose in the committee. One section of it was for following out the existing system,— for continuing the Arabic translations *, the profuse

* After all that had been expended on this object, there still remained 6,500*l.* assignèd for the completion of Arabic translations of only six books; viz. 3,200*l.* for five medical works, and 3,300*l.* for the untranslated part of Hutton's mathematics, " with something extra for diagrams." These ruinous expenses absorbed all our disposable funds, and starved the only useful branch of our operations, which was also the only one for which there was any real demand.

patronage of Arabic and Sanskrit works, and the printing operations; by all which means fresh masses would have been added to an already unsaleable and useless hoard. An edition of Avicenna was also projected, at an expense of 2,000*l.*; and as it was found that, after hiring students to attend the Arabic college, and having translations made for their use at an expense of thirty-two shillings a page, neither students nor teachers could understand them, it was proposed to employ the translator as the interpreter of his own writings, at a further expense of 300 rupees a month. The other section of the committee wished to dispense with this cumbrous and expensive machinery for teaching English science through the medium of the Arabic language; to give no bounties, in the shape of stipends to students, for the encouragement of any particular kind of learning; to purchase or print only such Arabic and Sanskrit books as might actually be required for the use of the different colleges; and to employ that portion of their annual income which would by these means be set free, in the establishment of new seminaries for giving instruction in English and the vernacular languages, at the places where such institutions were most in demand.

This fundamental difference of opinion long

obstructed the business of the committee. Almost
every thing which came before them was more or
less involved in it. The two parties were so
equally balanced as to be unable to make a forward movement in any direction. A particular
point might occasionally be decided by an acci-
dental majority of one or two, but as the decision
was likely to be reversed the next time the subject came under consideration, this only added inconsistency to inefficiency. This state of things
lasted for about three years, until both parties
became convinced that the usefulness and respectability of their body would be utterly compro-
mised by its longer continuance. The committee
had come to a dead stop, and the government
alone could set it in motion again, by giving a
preponderance to one or the other of the two
opposite sections. The members, therefore, took
the only course which remained open to them, and
laid before the government a statement of their
existing position, and of the grounds of the conflicting opinions held by them.

The question was now fairly brought to issue,
and the government was forced to make its elec-
tion between two opposite principles. So much,
perhaps, never depended upon the determination
of any government. Happily there was then at

the head of affairs one of the few who pursue the welfare of the public independently of every personal consideration: happily also he was supported by one who, after having embellished the literature of Europe, came to its aid when it was trembling in the scale with the literature of Asia. The decision which was come to is worthy of everlasting record. Although homely in its words, it will be mighty in its effects long after we are mouldering in the dust. It was as follows:—

" *Resolution of Government, dated 7th March* 1835.

" The governor general of India in council has attentively considered the two letters from the secretary to the committee, dated the 21st and 22d January last, and the papers referred to in them.

" 2d.—His lordship in council is of opinion that the great object of the British government ought to be the promotion of European literature and science amongst the natives of India, and that all the funds appropriated for the purposes of education would be best employed on English education alone.

" 3d.—But it is not the intention of his lordship in council to abolish any college or school of native learning, while the native population shall appear to be inclined to avail themselves of the advantages which it affords; and his lordship in council directs that all the existing professors and students at all the institutions under the superintendence of the committee shall continue to receive their stipends. But his lordship in council decidedly objects to the practice which has hitherto prevailed, of supporting the students during the period of their education. He conceives that the only effect of such a system can be to give artificial encouragement to branches of learning which, in the natural course of things, would be superseded by more useful studies; and he directs that no stipend shall be given to any student who may hereafter enter at any of these institutions, and that when any professor of oriental learning shall vacate his situation, the committee shall report to the government the number and state of the class, in order that the government may be able to decide upon the expediency of appointing a successor.

" 4th.—It has come to the knowledge of the governor general in council that a large sum has been expended by the committee in the printing of oriental works. His lordship in council directs that no portion of the funds shall hereafter be so employed.

" 5th.—His lordship in council directs, that all the funds which these reforms will leave at the disposal of the committee be henceforth employed in imparting to the native population a knowledge of English literature and science, through the medium of the English language; and his lordship in council requests the committee to submit to government with all expedition a plan for the accomplishment of this purpose.

" (A true copy.)
" (Signed)   H. T. PRINSEP,
" Sec^y to Government."

This decision was followed by a series of corresponding measures. The former president of the committee, seeing the turn affairs were taking, had handsomely offered to resign in favor of any one whose views were more in accordance with the prevailing opinions, continuing however to render very valuable assistance as a member of the committee.* Mr. Macaulay had been appointed to the vacant post. Two of the members most warmly attached to the oriental side of the question now gave in their resignation, and several new members were appointed, whose views coin-

* Intelligence has lately reached England of the death of Mr. Henry Shakespear, the gentleman alluded to; and I feel a melancholy pleasure in recording a circumstance so remarkably illustrating the spirit of equity and of quiet unobtrusive public feeling which breathed through all his actions. India did not contain a more amiable or excellent man.

cided with those of the government. The natives
also were now for the first time admitted to take
a share in the deliberations on the subject of
national instruction. This was done by conferring
on the managers of the Hindu college the privilege of electing two of their number in rotation
as members of the committee, and a Mohammedan
gentleman was soon after appointed a member of it.
Six new seminaries were immediately established
with a portion of the fund which had been placed
at the disposal of the committee by the cessation of
the Arabic and Sanskrit printing and translating,
and six more were established at the commencement
of the following year. Rules were devised for bringing the proceedings in the provincial seminaries periodically under the review of the general committee, and for stimulating exertion by rewarding the
most deserving students. It was resolved to annex
a good library to each seminary, and a large supply of books suited to all ages was ordered from
England. By permitting every body to make use
of the books on payment of a fixed subscription,
these libraries have become the means of diffusing knowledge much beyond the immediate
circle of the government seminaries, and being
now objects of general interest, many valuable
contributions are from time to time made to

them.* Scientific apparatus of various kinds was ordered from England. Professor Peacock, of Trinity college, Cambridge, at the request of the committee, selected and sent out the mathematical class books required at the different institutions. Arrangements were made with the school-book society for the publication of a book of selections from the English poets, from Chaucer downwards, and the expediency of publishing a corresponding volume in prose is now under consideration.

When these operations commenced there were fourteen seminaries under the control of the Committee: there are now forty. At the first-mentioned period there were about 3,398 pupils, of whom 1,818 were learning English, 218 Arabic, and 473 Sanskrit. There are now upwards of 6,000. The number of Sanskrit and Arabic students is smaller than before. A small number study Persian, or learn the vernacular language only; all the rest receive an English education. The seminary which was last established completely exhausted the funds at the disposal of the

---

* As most young men take out a stock of books with them to India, while few bring any back, the common English standard works have accumulated there to a great extent. The public libraries which have been established by the committee in the principal towns form a nucleus round which these and many other books collect.

committee. It was for the district of Dinajpoor, which is computed to contain 6,000 square miles, above 12,000 towns and villages, and a population exceeding 2,300,000; and it is a district remarkable even in Bengal for the darkness of the ignorance which prevails in it. Though many of the leading inhabitants concurred with the European authorities in desiring that some effectual steps should be taken to enlighten this part of the country, the utmost the committee was able to afford was seventy rupees a month.

As the general superintendence of the system is vested in a " general committee," residing at Calcutta, so the management of each particular seminary is intrusted to a local committee residing on the spot. The members of these committees are appointed by the government from all classes of the community, native as well as European. Care is taken in the selection to secure for the support of the system as much zeal, influence, and information as possible, and nobody who has the cause at heart, and can really aid it, need be without a share in the management. It is the wish of the general committee to employ the government fund only in the payment of the salaries of teachers; by this means the permanence of the institutions will be secured, at the same time that full scope will be left for the exercise of private munificence; and as the outlay of the committee will be confined to fixed payments, easily susceptible of control, no inconvenience will be likely to ensue from the wide extension of the system. The pupils themselves are expected to pay for the ordinary school-books used by them, and it is intended to demand a small fixed sum in part of payment for their instruction. More regular attendance is thus secured; nominal students, who injure the discipline and retard the progress of the institutions, become rare; the system is raised in general estimation, and additional means are acquired for improving and extending it. Boarding-houses are beginning to be established in connection with some of the seminaries, for the accommodation of pupils who reside at a distance.

In all the new institutions the important principle has been established of admitting boys of every caste without distinction. A different practice prevailed in the older institutions; the Sanskrit colleges were appropriated to Brahmins; the Arabic colleges, with a few exceptions, to Mohammedans; and even at the Anglo-Indian institution, which goes by the name of the Hindu college, none but Hindus of good caste were admitted. This practice was found to encourage the prejudice which it was meant to conciliate. The opposite practice has been attended with no inconvenience of any kind; Christian, Mohammedan, and Hindu boys, of every shade of colour and variety of descent, may be seen standing side by side in the same class, engaged in the common pursuit of English literature, contending for the same honours, and forced to acknowledge the existence of superior merit in their comrades of the lowest, as well as in those of the highest caste. This is a great point gained. The artificial institution of caste cannot long survive the period when the youth of India, instead of being trained to observe it, shall be led by the daily habit of their lives to disregard it. All we have to do is to bring them together, to impress the same character on them, and to leave the yielding and affectionate mind of youth to its natural impulse. Habits of friendly communication will thus be established between all classes, they will insensibly become one people, and the process of enlightening our subjects will proceed simultaneously with that of uniting them among themselves.

In the long discussions which preceded the change in the plan of the committee, there was one point on which all parties were agreed: this was, that the vernacular languages contained neither the literary nor scientific information necessary for a liberal education. It was admitted on all sides that while the instruction of the mass of the people through the medium of their own language was the ultimate object to be kept in view, yet, meanwhile, teachers had to be trained, a literature had to be created, and the co-operation of the upper and middle classes of native society had to be secured. The question which divided the committee was, What language was the best instrument for the accomplishment of these great objects? Half the members contended that it was English, the other half that it was Sanskrit and Arabic. As there was no dispute about the vernacular language, no mention was made of it in the resolution of the 7th March 1835, which contained the decision of the government. This omission led many, who were not acquainted with the course the discussion had taken, to fear that the point had been altogether overlooked; and in order to obviate this misapprehension the committee made the following remarks, in the first annual report submitted by them to the government after the promulgation of the resolution referred to : —

" We are deeply sensible of the importance of encouraging the cultivation of the vernacular languages. We do not conceive that the order of the 7th of March precludes us from doing this, and we have constantly acted on this construction. In the discussions which preceded that order, the claims of the vernacular languages were broadly and prominently admitted by all parties, and the question submitted for the decision of government, only concerned the relative advantage of teaching English on the one side, and the learned eastern languages on the other. We therefore conceive that the phrases ' European literature and science,' ' English education alone,' and ' imparting to the native population a knowledge of English literature and science through the medium of the English language,' are intended merely to secure the preference to European learning taught through the medium of the English language, over oriental learning taught through the medium of the Sanskrit and Arabic languages, as regards the instruction of those natives who receive a learned education at our seminaries. These expressions have, as we understand them, no reference to the question through what ulterior medium such instruction as the mass of the people is capable of receiving, is to be conveyed. If Eng-

lish had been rejected, and the learned eastern
tongues adopted, the people must equally have
received their knowledge through the vernacular
dialects. It was therefore quite unnecessary for
the government, in deciding the question between
the rival languages, to take any notice of the vernacular tongues, and consequently we have thought
that nothing could reasonably be inferred from its
omission to take such notice.

" We conceive the formation of a vernacular
literature to be the ultimate object to which all
our efforts must be directed. At present, the extensive cultivation of some foreign language, which
is always very improving to the mind, is rendered
indispensable by the almost total absence of a
vernacular literature, and the consequent impossi-
bility of obtaining a tolerable education from that
source only. The study of English, to which many
circumstances induce the natives to give the preference, and with it the knowledge of the learning
of the west, is therefore daily spreading. This, as
it appears to us, is the first stage in the process
by which India is to be enlightened. The natives
must learn before they can teach. The best educated among them must be placed in possession of
our knowledge, before they can transfer it into
their own language. We trust that the number

of such translations will now multiply every year. As the superiority of European learning becomes more generally appreciated, the demand for them will no doubt increase, and we shall be able to encourage any good books which may be brought out in the native languages by adopting them extensively in our seminaries.

" A teacher of the vernacular language of the province is already attached to several of our institutions, and we look to this plan soon becoming general. We have also endeavoured to secure the means of judging for ourselves of the degree of attention which is paid to this important branch of instruction, by requiring that the best translations from English into the vernacular language, and vice versâ, should be sent to us after each annual examination, and if they seem to deserve it, a pecuniary prize is awarded by us to the authors of them."

These views were entirely approved by the government, and have since been steadily acted upon by the committee. One or more teachers of the vernacular language of the district form a regular part of the establishment of each English school, (at the Hoogly college there are as many as ten,) and pains are taken to give the pupils the habit of writing it with facility and propriety.

The instructions to the local committees on this
head are, " that the pupils should be constantly
exercised in translating into their own language,
as well as into English, from the time they enter
the seminaries till their departure; and that
they should also practise original composition in
both languages as soon as their minds have
been sufficiently opened to attempt it with ad
vantage."

The revenue authorities took advantage of the
establishment of the new provincial seminaries to
carry into effect a plan, which had beenpreviously
attempted without success, for securing a proper
education for the numerous wards of the government. Rules were laid down for this purpose.
The wards are either to be brought up at the
nearest seminary, or to be provided with tutors
and books for their instruction at their own homes.
Their attention is to be particularly directed to
those branches of knowledge which have an obvious bearing on the good management and improvement of their estates; and their progress in
their studies is to be periodically tested and reported on. There is, perhaps, no part of the
world where so much wealth and influence is possessed by persons so little able to make a good use

of it as in the interior of Bengal.* The substitution of a single humane and enlightened landlord would be a blessing to a whole neighbourhood. The elevation of the character of the whole class would be a national benefit of the first magnitude. A great deal has been said about the advantage of having English landholders, but till lately nothing has been done to render the native landholders, who must always be the majority, more fit for the performance of their duties. In Bengal, owing to the indolent and intemperate habits, and consequent early deaths of many of the great zemindars, minorities are frequent, and a large proportion of the landed property of the country falls under the management of the government in the course of a few years. In the western provinces, where landed property exists in a more wholesome form, a new settlement for thirty years has given peace of mind, leisure, and comparative opulence to the agricultural classes. If these circumstances are

---

* As by the permanent settlement we have put the agricultural classes into the hands of the Bengal zemindars, we are bound, as far as we are able, to qualify the latter to exercise their power aright. The new men who have purchased their estates under our system are, as a class, friendly to improvement; but when they take up their abode in parts of the country where there are no means of obtaining a tolerable education, they become after a generation or two as ignorant and bigoted as the rest.

properly taken advantage of, we shall ere long be able to make a salutary impression on this most important part of the community.

While the general question of native education was debated in the committee, a distinct but deeply interesting branch of the subject under-went a similar examination elsewhere. The in-struction of the natives in the medical art had hitherto been provided for as follows. The sys-tems of Galen and Hippocrates, and of the Shasters, with the addition of a few scraps of European medical science, was taught in classes which had been attached for that purpose to the Arabic and Sanskrit colleges at Calcutta. There was also a separate institution at Calcutta, the object of which was to train up " native doctors," or assistants to the European medical officers. There was only one teacher attached to this in-stitution, and he delivered his lectures in Hin-dusthanee. The only medical books open to the pupils were a few short tracts which had been translated for their use into that language; the only dissection practised was that of the inferior animals. It is obvious that the knowledge com-municated by such imperfect means could neither be complete nor practical.

Much public benefit had been derived in the

judicial and revenue administration from the substitution of cheap native, for dear European agency. Lord William Bentinck now proposed to extend this plan to the medical department, and to raise up a class of native medical practitioners, educated on sound European principles, to supersede the native quacks who, unacquainted with anatomy or the simplest principles of chemical action, prey on the people, and hesitate not to use the most dangerous drugs and poisons. Physicians and surgeons, however, were not to be had ready-made, like judges and collectors. A professional education was necessary, and it was doubtful whether the natives would submit to the conditions which this education implied. A committee was therefore appointed to inquire into and report on the subject.

After a careful investigation, the committee came to the conclusion that it was perfectly feasible to educate native medical men on broad European principles, some of whom might be gradually substituted for the foreign practitioners at the civil and military stations, and others might be sent out among the mass of their countrymen, to give them the inestimable blessing of enlightened medical attendance. With regard to practical human anatomy, they stated it as their opinion

that " times are much changed, and the difficulties that stood in the way appear no longer
insurmountable;" and they considered a knowledge
of the English language to be a necessary previous
qualification in the pupils, " because that language
combines within itself the circle of all the sciences,
and incalculable wealth of printed works and
illustrations; circumstances that give it obvious
advantages over the oriental languages, in which
are only to be found the crudest elements of
science, or the most irrational substitutes for it."

This point, however, was not attained without
encountering a sharp opposition. The superintendent of the medical institution, a learned and
enthusiastic orientalist, set in array the arguments
of his party, and confidently predicted the failure
of every attempt to remodel the institution on the
principles advocated by the medical committee.
The Rev. Mr. (now Doctor) Duff, to whom the
cause of sound learning and true religion in the
East is deeply indebted, took up the opposite side.
The battle which had been so well contested in
the education committee was fought over again
in this new field; but I must refer to the extract
from the medical committee's report in the appendix for the substance of what was said on both
sides.

In accordance with the recommendation of this committee, the old medical institution and the Arabic and Sanskrit medical classes were abolished, and an entirely new college was founded, in which the various branches of medical science cultivated in Europe are taught on the most approved European system. The establishment of professors, the library, the museum, are on the most liberal scale. A hospital is about to be opened on the premises belonging to the college, for the purpose of giving the students the advantage of clinical instruction. Distinguished pupils are drafted from the different provincial seminaries to the medical college, and it is intended to establish dispensaries, including the necessary provision for vaccination and for the treatment of surgical cases, at the principal towns in the interior, which will be placed under the charge of young men who have been educated at the college. European medical science will thus strike root at once in many different parts of Gangetic India, and the knowledge acquired at the new institution will be employed from the earliest possible period in alleviating the sufferings of the people. Of all the late measures for the promotion of education in India, this alone was adopted in anticipation of the effectual demand; and the stipends, which had always been

allowed to medical students, must therefore be
continued until the advantages to be derived from
the college by persons wishing to qualify themselves for the medical profession become more
generally evident. The professional training at
that institution is carried so much beyond the
period usually allotted to education in India, that,
without this assistance, the poverty or indifference
of the parents would often cause the studies of
the young men, particularly when they come from
a distance, to be brought to a premature close.

This noble institution is succeeding to the full
extent of the most sanguine expectations which
had been formed of it. The pupils are animated
by the most lively professional zeal, and they
evince a degree of quickness and intelligence in
the prosecution of their studies which has perhaps
never been surpassed. Mr. James Prinsep, who
tested the proficiency of the chemical class at the
last examination, reported officially as follows:—
" In the first place, I may remark generally, that
all the essays are extremely creditable. Indeed,
the extent and accuracy of the information on
the single subject selected to test the abilities
of the pupils has far surpassed my expectations;
and I do not think that in Europe any class of
chemical pupils would be found capable of passing

a better examination for the time they have attended lectures, nor, indeed, that an equal number
of boys would be found so nearly on a par in their
acquirements. The differences are those rather
of different age, different natural ability, or reten-
tion of memory. The faults of explanation are
trifling. Grammatical errors are more numerous,
but allowance must be made for them in boys
writing in a foreign tongue, in the rudiments of
which they have been unequally instructed.

" Many of the papers show that, besides at-
tending to the words of the lecturer, the writers
have studied his manual,—indeed some seem almost
to use his very words; but I by no means regard
this as a fault; on the contrary, it proves attention
and interest in the subject of their studies. One
or two go farther, and quote other authorities, to
which they must have had recourse in their
reading up; and as it could not be known what
subject would be placed before them, this betokens
a considerable acquaintance with chemical authors.
One pupil, indeed, details the whole series of toxi-
cological tests for discovering arsenical poisons;
and I should be inclined to award the highest
place to him, were there not some inaccuracies in
his too brief notice of the general properties of
the metal." Mr. James Prinsep is secretary to

the Asiatic Society, and is well known for his scientific attainments. His testimony is the more gratifying, because he is attached to the oriental class of opinions, and was one of the two members who seceded from the committee when it was resolved to take a decided course in favour of English.

The peculiar glory of the medical college, however, consists in the victory which it has obtained over the most intractable of the national prejudices, which often survives a change of religion, and was supposed to be interwoven, if any thing could be, with the texture itself of the Hindu mind. Brahmins and other high-caste Hindus may be seen in the dissecting-room of the college handling the knife, and demonstrating from the human subject, with even more than the indifference of European professional men. Operations at the sight of which English students not unfrequently faint, are regarded with the most eager interest, and without any symptom of loathing, by the self-possessed Hindu. Subjects for dissection are easily and unobjectionably obtained in a country in which human life is more than usually precarious, and where the respect felt for the dead is much less than in Europe. An injection of arsenic into the veins prevents that rapid decomposition which the heat of the climate would otherwise engender. There is now nothing to prevent the people of India from attaining to the highest eminence in the medical art; and we shall soon be able to make the college entirely national, by replacing the foreign by indigenous professors. The importance of this remarkable step in the progress of native improvement is so generally acknowledged, that even the Hindus of the old school have given in their adherence to the medical college; and the Shasters, with the elasticity peculiar to them, have been made to declare that the dissection of human bodies for medical purposes is not prohibited by them. The establishment of the medical college has received the approbation of the Court of Directors; they have indeed reason to be proud of it as one of the chief ornaments of their administration.

Besides settling the principle of national education, Lord William Bentinck prepared the means of ultimately extending it to the mass of the people. He justly considered that, to place this great work on a solid foundation, it was necessary to ascertain the exact nature and extent of the popular wants, the difficulties and the facilities of the task, and the local peculiarities which might require a partial change of plan. Our knowledge of the existing state of feeling and of mental cultivation in the principal towns was sufficiently accurate to enable us to proceed with confidence, as far as they were concerned; but more minute information was necessary before we could venture to extend our operations from town to country, from the few with whom the European society are in direct communication to the body of the people. Mr. William Adam, a gentleman distinguished for his accurate and methodical habits of mind, and for his intimate acquaintance with the natives and their languages, was therefore appointed to make a searching inquiry into the existing state of native education in the interior. Mr. Adam has ever since been employed on his educational survey, and has visited many different districts, average specimens of which he has subjected to a strict analysis.

Meanwhile all the materials of a national system of education are fast accumulating; teachers are trained; books are multiplied; the interest felt in the subject is strengthening and spreading; and the upper class of natives in the towns are being prepared to aid by their influence and example in the enlightening of the lower classes in the country.

CHAP. II.

The Study of Foreign Languages and Literature a powerful Instrument of National Improvement. — The Instruction of the upper and middle Classes the first Object.

THE past history of the world authorizes us to believe that the movement which is taking place in India, if properly directed and supported by the Government, will end in bringing about a decided change for the better in the character of the people. The instances in which nations have worked their way to a high degree of civilization from domestic resources only are extremely rare, compared with those in which the impulse has been communicated from without, and has been supported by the extensive study and imitation of the literature of foreign countries. The cases in which the most lasting impressions have been made upon national character, in which the superior civilization of one country, has taken deepest root and fructified most abundantly in other countries, have a strong general resemblance to the case before us. In those cases the foreign systems of learning were first studied in the original tongue by the upper and middle classes, who alone

possessed the necessary leisure. From this followed a diffusion of the knowledge contained in
the foreign literature, a general inclination of the
national taste towards it, and an assimilation of
the vernacular language, by the introduction into
it of numerous scientific and other terms. Last
of all, the vernacular tongue began to be cultivated in its improved state; translations and imitations sprang up in abundance, and creative
genius occasionally caught the impulse, and struck
out a masterpiece of its own.

Every scholar knows to what a great extent the
Romans cultivated Grecian literature, and adopted
Grecian models of taste. It was only after the
national mind had become deeply impregnated
from this source, that they began to have a literature of their own. The writers of the Augustan
age were bred in the school, were animated by the
spirit, were nourished with the food of conquered
Greece. Virgil was a mere imitator, however
noble : the Roman dramas are feeble translations from the Greek : the entire Roman literature is only an echo of the Greek literature.
The Romans made no scruple in acknowledging
the obligations they were under to the cultivation
of Grecian learning. Their enthusiasm was directed to the object of enriching their native

language with all that, in that age of the world,
could be imported from abroad.

It is a curious fact that an intellectual revolution similar to that which is now in progress in
India, actually took place among the Romans.
At an early period, the Etruscan was, as Livy tells
us, the language which the young Romans studied.
No patrician was considered as liberally educated
who had not learned in the sacred books of the
augurs of Clusium and Volaterræ, how to quarter
the heavens, what was meant by the appearance
of a vulture on the left hand, and what rites were
to be performed on a spot which had been smitten
by thunder. This sort of knowledge — very ana-
lagous to the knowledge which is contained in the
Sanskrit books, — was considered as the most
valuable learning, until an increased acquaintance
with the Greek language produced a complete
change. Profound speculations on morals, legis
lation, and government; lively pictures of human
life and manners; pure and energetic models of
political eloquence, drove out the jargon of a
doting superstition. If we knew more minutely
the history of that change, we should probably
find that it was vehemently resisted by very distinguished Etruscan scholars, and that all sorts of
fearful consequences were represented as inevit-

able, if the old learning about the flight of birds and the entrails of beasts should be abandoned for Homer, and if the mysteries of the *bidental* should be neglected for Thucydides and Plato.

The Roman language and literature, thus enriched and improved, was destined to still prouder triumphs. The inhabitants of the greatest part of Europe and of the North of Africa, educated in every respect like the Romans, became in every respect equal to them. The impression which was then made will never be effaced. It sank so deep into the language and habits of the people, that Latin to this day forms the basis of the tongues of France and southern Europe, and the Roman law the basis of their jurisprudence. The barbarous hordes which triumphed over the arms, yielded to the arts of Rome. Roman literature survived the causes which led to its diffusion, and even spread beyond the ancient limits of the empire. The Poles and Hungarians were led neither by any pressure from without, nor by any artificial encouragement from within, to make Latin their language of education, of literature, of business, and, to a very remarkable extent, of ordinary colloquial intercourse. They did so, we may presume, because their own language contained nothing worth knowing, while Latin included within itself

almost all the knowledge which at that time existed in the world.

After this came the great revival of learning,
at the close of the fifteenth and the beginning
of the sixteenth centuries. At that period, the
historian Robertson observes, " all the modern
languages were in a state extremely barbarous, devoid of elegance, of vigour, and even
of perspicuity. No author thought of writing
in language so ill adapted to express and embellish his sentiments, or of erecting a work for
immortality with such rude and perishable materials. As the spirit which prevailed at that time
did not owe its rise to any original effort of the
human mind, but was excited chiefly by admira-
tion of the ancients, which began then to be
studied with attention in every part of Europe,
their compositions were deemed not only the
standards of taste and of sentiment, but of style;
and even the languages in which they wrote were
thought to be peculiar, and almost consecrated to
learning and the muses. Not only the manner of
the ancients was imitated, but their language was
adopted; and, extravagant as the attempt may
appear, to write in a dead tongue, in which men
were not accustomed to think, and which they
could not speak, or even pronounce, the success

of it was astonishing. As they formed their style upon the purest models; as they were uninfected with those barbarisms, which the inaccuracy of familiar conversation, the affectation of courts, intercourse with strangers, and a thousand other causes, introduce into living languages, many moderns have attained to a degree of elegance in their Latin compositions which the Romans themselves scarce possessed beyond the limits of the Augustan age."

Had the mental stimulus produced by the revival of letters been confined to scholars, the progress of improvement would have stopped at this point; but all who had time to read, whether they knew Latin or not, felt the influence of the movement, and this great class was receiving continual additions from the rapid increase of wealth. Hence arose a demand which the classical languages could not satisfy, and from this demand sprang the vernacular literature of Europe. We are indebted to foreign nations and distant ages both for the impulse which struck it out, and for the writings which warmed the fancy and formed the taste of its founders. Abounding, as we are, in intellectual wealth, could we venture even now to tell our youth that they have no longer occasion to seek for nourishment from the stores of the Latin, Greek, French, German, Spanish, and Italian literatures? The French fell into a mistake of this kind, and they have suffered for it. Proud of the honour, and sensible of the political advantage of having their own language generally understood, they were not sufficiently alive to the new resources they might have derived from the study of foreign languages.* Their literature, therefore, wants that copiousness and variety which is characteristic of the English and German. Now they see their error, and, instead of confining themselves to their own stores, and copying and re-copying their own models, they have begun to look abroad and study the master-pieces of other nations. German literature is a remarkable instance of the success with which industry and genius may nationalize foreign materials. It has arisen, almost within the memory of persons now living, on the basis of the astonishing erudition collected by the German writers from every living and dead language worth laying under contribution.

Had our ancestors acted as the committee of pub-

* It has been justly observed, that for the French to pride themselves upon all foreign nations studying their language, while they study the language of no foreign nation, is like a blind man boasting that every body can see him, while he can see nobody.

lic instruction acted up to March 1835*; "had they neglected the language of Thucydides and Plato, and the language of Cicero and Tacitus; had they confined their attention to the old dialects of our own island; had they printed nothing and taught nothing at the universities but chronicles in Anglo-Saxon, and romances in Norman French, would England ever have been what she now is? What the Greek and Latin were to the contemporaries of More and Ascham, our tongue is to the people of India. The literature of England is now more valuable than that of classical antiquity. I doubt whether the Sanskrit literature be as valuable as that of our Saxon and Norman progenitors; in some departments, in history, for example, I am certain that it is much less so.

Another instance may be said to be still before our eyes. Within the last hundred and twenty years a nation, which had previously been in a state as barbarous as that in which our ancestors were before the crusades, has gradually emerged from the ignorance in which it was sunk, and has taken its place among civilized communities. I speak of Russia. There is now in that country a

---

* This is taken from one of the papers recorded during the discussions which preceded the resolution of the 7th March 1835. I shall hereafter make several similar extracts.

large educated class, abounding with persons fit
to serve the state in the highest functions, and in
nowise inferior to the most accomplished men
who adorn the best circles of Paris and London.
There is reason to hope that this vast empire,
which in the time of our grandfathers was probably behind the Punjab, may in the time of
of our grandchildren be pressing close on
France and Britain in the career of improvement. And how was this change effected? Not
by flattering national prejudices; not by feeding
the mind of the young Muscovite with the old
women's stories which his rude fathers had believed; not by filling his head with lying legends
about St. Nicholas; not by encouraging him to
study the great question, whether the world was
or was not created on the 13th of September; not
by calling him " a learned native " when he had
mastered all these points of knowledge; but by
teaching him those foreign languages in which the
greatest mass of information had been laid up,
and thus putting all that information within his
reach. The languages of western Europe civilized
Russia. I cannot doubt that they will do for the
Hindoo what they have done for the Tartar."

The literary epoch of the Arabians dates from
the time at which they commenced the study of the

Grecian writers. That the impulse was not stronger or more permanent, is owing, perhaps, to the partial use which they made of this great instrument of national improvement. If, instead of contenting themselves with meagre translations of some of the Greek philosophers, they had studied Plato and Xenophon, Homer and Thucydides, in the original, a flame of generous liberty might have been kindled, and a new direction might have been given at that period to the views and feelings of the people of the East, the possible effects of which up to the present day it is impossible to calculate. * The Arabs pursued a very different course in

* Gibbon observes on this point:—" The Moslems deprived themselves of the principal benefits of a familiar intercourse with Greece and Rome, the knowledge of antiquity, the purity of taste, and the freedom of thought. Confident in the riches of their native tongue, the Arabians disdained the study of any foreign idiom. The philosophers of Athens and Rome enjoyed the blessings and asserted the rights of civil and religious freedom. Their moral and political writings might have gradually unlocked the fetters of eastern despotism, diffused a liberal spirit of inquiry and toleration, and encouraged the Arabian sages to suspect that their caliph was a tyrant, and their prophet an impostor. To the thirst of martyrdom, the vision of paradise, and the belief of predestination, we must ascribe the invincible enthusiasm of the prince and people; and the sword of the Saracens became less formidable when their youth was drawn away from the camp to the college, when the armies of the faithful presumed to read and reflect. Yet the foolish vanity of the Greeks was jealous of their studies, and reluctantly imparted the sacred fire to the barbarians of the East." These Moslems were only the neighbours of the lower empire,

their intercourse with the various nations included
within their dominions. They extolled the beauty
of their own language, and gave the utmost encouragement to the cultivation of it. The effect
was not universally beneficial, because many of
the subject races were already in a more advanced
stage of civilization than the Arabs themselves;
but it was such as exemplified, in a very remarkable way, the extent to which the study of a new
language and literature may remould national
character. Arabic literature became the literature
of all the conquered nations; their dialects were
saturated with Arabic words; their habits of
thought, their manners, their whole character,
became conformed to the same standard. Religion has, no doubt, a great deal to do with the
striking uniformity which prevails throughout the
Mohammedan world; but language and literature
have a great deal more to do with it. There are
many tribes on the outskirts of Mohammedanism
which have conformed to the religion, without
adopting the learning of Islam, and they are often

and it was perhaps not in the power of the Greeks to make more
than a faint impression upon them. The Moslems with whom we
have to do are our own subjects; and if we neglect to mitigate the
hostile spirit of the sect, by encouraging the disposition they evince
to cultivate our literature and science, posterity will have a heavier
charge to bring against us than that of " foolish vanity."

not to be distinguished from the people of the same tribe who have adhered to the religion of their fathers, with whom they have language and every thing else in common.

These are the facts upon which the plan of the education committee is based. Their object is to fill the minds of the liberally educated portion of the people with the knowledge of Europe, in order that they may interpret it in their own language to the rest of their countrymen. For this purpose, while, on the one hand, the pupils are encouraged to acquire the various kinds of information which English literature contains, and to form their taste after the best English models; on the other, every endeavour is used to give them the habit of writing with facility and elegance in their native language.

The committee's first desire is to establish a seminary based on these principles at each Zillah station. The large towns always take the lead in the march of improvement: the class of people whose circumstances give them leisure to study to good purpose, and influence to make their example followed, are congregated there in greater numbers than elsewhere. Even the proprietors residing on their estates in the district keep up a close connection with their provincial capitals,

where they have generally town houses and resi-
dent agents.   The subordinate officers of government are selected and sent from thence to exercise their functions in the surrounding country.
The European functionaries are present there to
exercise a general superintendence over the seminaries, and to assist the teachers with their coun-
tenance and experience.   By purifying the circu-
lation through these vital organs, the whole system
will be re-invigorated; the rich, the learned, the
men of business, will first be gained; a new class
of teachers will be trained; books in the vernacular language will be multiplied; and with these
accumulated means we shall in due time proceed
to extend our operations from town to country,
from the few to the many, until every hamlet
shall be provided with its elementary school.
The poor man is not less the object of the committee's solicitude than the rich; but, while the
means at their disposal were extremely limited,
there were millions of all classes to be educated.
It was absolutely necessary to make a selection,
and they therefore selected the upper and middle
classes as the first object of their attention,
because, by educating them first, they would
soonest be able to extend the same advantages to
the rest of the people.   They will be our school-

masters, translators, authors; none of which functions the poor man, with his scanty stock of knowledge, is able to perform. They are the leaders
of the people. By adopting them first into our
system we shall be able to proceed a few years
hence, with an abundant supply of proper books
and instructors, and with all the wealth and influence of the country on our side, to establish a
general system of education which shall afford to
every person of every rank the means of acquiring that degree of knowledge which his leisure
will permit.

CHAP. III.

The violent Opposition made by Oriental Scholars to the Resolution of the 7th March 1835. — The whole Question rests upon Two Points ; first, Whether English or Arabic and Sanskrit Literature is best calculated for the Improvement of the People of India ; and secondly, Whether, supposing English Literature to be best adapted for that Purpose, the Natives are willing to cultivate it. — These Points considered.

THE resolution of the 7th of March 1835 was passed in the face of the most keen and determined opposition on the part of several distinguished persons whose influence had not been usually exerted in vain; and their representations were seconded by a petition got up by the numerous class of persons whose subsistence was dependent on the oriental colleges, and on the printing and other operations of the committee connected with them. The Asiatic Society also took up the cause with great vehemence, and memorialised the local government, while the Court of Directors and the Board of Control were pressed by strong remonstrances from the Royal Asiatic Society. The spirit of orientalism was stirred up to its inmost depths, and the cry of indignation of the Calcutta literati was re-echoed with more than its original bitterness from the colleges of France and Germany.

In order to understand these phenomena, it will be necessary to go back a few years in the history of India. When Lord Wellesley established the college of Fort William, he provided munificently for the encouragement of oriental learning. For a long time after, that learning was nearly the sole test of merit among the junior members of the civil service, and such military and medical officers as aspired to civil employment. (A superior knowledge of Sanskrit and Arabic was sure to be rewarded by a good place. The reputations of many members of the government and of nearly all the secretaries had been founded on this basis. The literary circle of Calcutta was almost exclusively composed of orientalists. The education committee was formed when this state of things was at its height, and hence the decidedly oriental cast of its first proceedings.

By degrees the rage for orientalism subsided among the Europeans, while the taste for European literature rose to a great height among the natives. A modification of the committee's proceedings suited to this altered state of things was called for; but the persons who had been trained under the

old system still occupied the strongholds of the
administration, and motives were not wanting to
dispose them to an obstinate defence. The habits
of a long life were now for the first time broken
in upon. They felt as if the world were given to
understand that they had spent their strength for
nought, and that their learning was altogether
vanity.* The axe seemed to them to be laid at
the root of their reputations. This was more than
human nature could bear. Men who had been
remarkable for self-restraint completely lost their
temper, and those who had been accustomed to
give free expression to their feelings showed unusual warmth on this occasion. It was a striking
exhibition of character. It is true that the well-
earned honours of mature life had rendered several of these distinguished persons independent

* Jacquemont makes the following remarks on this subject in
one of his letters to his father, vol. i. p. 222-3 : — " Le Sanskrit
ne ménera à rien qu'au Sanskrit. Le méchanisme de ce langage
est admirablement compliqué, et néanmoins, dit on, admirable.
Mais c'est comme une de ces machines qui ne sortent pas de con-
servatoires et des muséums, plus ingenieuses qu'utiles. Elle n'à
servi qu'à fabriquer de la théologie, de la métaphysique, de l'his-
toire mêlée de théologie, et autres billevésées du même genre :
galimathias triple pour les faiseurs et pour les consommateurs,
pour les consommateurs étrangers surtout, galimathias ⅓, &c. &c.
La mode du Sanskrit et de l'orientalisme littéraire en général durera
cependant, parce que ceux qui avront passé ou perdu quinze ou
vingt ans à apprendre l'Arabe ou le Sanskrit n'auront la candeur
d'avouer qu'ils possèdent une science inutile."

of their early reputation for eastern learning.
But this availed nothing. The blow had gone
straight to the sources of their habitual feelings, and the effect which followed was highly
remarkable.

The motive which led the oriental literary societies to take up the cause of that section of the
committee which supported the interests of oriental
literature is still more obvious. The object of the
Asiatic societies is to investigate the history and
antiquities of the East; to lay open to the European
world whatever the records of Asia contain to
illustrate and aid the progress of mind, of morals,
and of natural history. The object of the education committee is to instruct the people of India in
sound knowledge and true morality. The Asiatic
societies are organs for making known the arts
and sciences of Asia to Europe.) The education
committee is an organ for making known the arts
and sciences of Europe to Asia. Yet different, and,
to a great extent, incompatible, as these objects are, the education committee had acted, in
the main, as if it had been only a subordinate
branch of the Bengal Asiatic Society. The same
gentleman was long secretary to both. Ancient
learning of a kind which every body must admit

to be more fit for an antiquarian society than for a seminary of popular education was profusely patronised. Extensive plans for the publication of Arabic and Sanskrit works, which exceeded the means of any literary association, were executed out of the fund which the British parliament had assigned for enlightening the people of India. The full extent of this union became apparent after it had been dissolved. A limb had been torn from the parent trunk, and the struggle with which the disruption was resisted showed how intimate the connection had been. By vehemently complaining of the suspension of the plans for the encouragement of ancient oriental literature, the literary societies virtually acknowledged the identity of their own operations and of the past operations of the education committee.

Those societies are entitled to the highest respect, and nobody can blame them for endeavouring to obtain support in the prosecution of the laudable objects for which they are associated. The responsible parties were the education committee and the Bengal government. It was for them to consider whether the mode which had been adopted of disbursing the education fund was the one best suited to the accomplishment of the object for which that fund had been instituted. If it was, they had properly acquitted themselves of the trust reposed in them, whether their plans happened to coincide with those of the Asiatic Society or not; if it was not, some change was obviously required.

This deeply important subject was long and carefully examined, both by the committee and the government. The decision which was come to has been already related, and it is needless to recount all the arguments which were used on the occasion. The whole question turns upon two points: the first of which is, whether English or Sanskrit and Arabic literature is best calculated for the enlightenment of the people of India; the other, whether, supposing English literature to be best adapted for that purpose, the natives are ready to avail themselves of the advantages which it holds out. When these points are determined the question is settled, and it is capable of being settled in no other way.

The comparative state of science in European and Asiatic countries might be supposed to be too well known to admit of any dispute on the first point; but as our opponents sometimes argue as if it were still a doubtful question whether English or oriental literature is most calculated to advance

the cause of human improvement, I shall appeal
to several authorities which will, I think, be listened
to with deference on this question.

The pains which the late Bishop Heber took to
obtain correct information on every subject which
had even a remote bearing on the improvement of
India are so well known, that nobody will be surprised at his having left his opinion on this vital
point fully on record.   The following is extracted
from his letter to Sir Wilmot Horton, dated March
1824, published in the appendix to his journal.

" Government has, however, been very liberal
in its grants, both to a society for national education, and in the institution and support of two
colleges of Hindu students of riper age, the one
at Benares, the other at Calcutta.   But I do not
think any of these institutions, in the way after
which they are at present conducted, likely to do
much good.   In the elementary schools supported
by the former, through a very causeless and ridiculous fear of giving offence to the natives, they
have forbidden the use of the Scriptures or any
extracts from them, though the moral lessons of
the Gospel are read by all Hindus who can get
hold of them, without scruple, and with much
attention, and though their exclusion is tanta-
mount to excluding all moral instruction from

their schools, the Hindu sacred writings having nothing of the kind, and, if they had, being shut up from the majority of the people by the double fence of a dead language, and an actual prohibition to read them, as too holy for common eyes or ears. The defects of the latter will appear when I have told you that the actual state of Hindu and Mussulman literature, mutatis mutandis, very nearly resembles what the literature of Europe was before the time of Galileo, Copernicus, and Bacon. The Mussulmans take their logic from Aristotle, filtered through many successive translations and commentaries, and their metaphysical system is professedly derived from Plato, (' Filatoun'). The Hindus have systems not very dissimilar from these, though, I am told, of greater length and more intricacy; but the studies in which they spend most of their time are the acquisition of the Sanskrit, and the endless refinements of its grammar, prosody, and poetry. Both have the same natural philosophy, which is also that of Aristotle in zoology and botany, and Ptolemy in astronomy, for which the Hindus have forsaken their more ancient notions of the seven seas, the six earths, and the flat base of Padalon, supported on the back of a tortoise. By the science which they now possess they are some of them able to foretell an eclipse, or compose an almanac; and many of them derive some little pecuniary advantage from pretensions to judicial astrology. In medicine and chemistry they are just sufficiently advanced to talk of substances being moist, dry, hot, &c. in the third or fourth degree; to dissuade from letting blood or physicking on a Tuesday, or under a particular aspect of the heavens, and to be eager in their pursuit of the philosopher's stone, and the elixir of immortality.

" The task of enlightening the studious youth of such a nation would seem to be a tolerably straightforward one. But though, for the college in Calcutta, (not Bishop's College, remember, but the Sanskrit, or Hindu College,) an expensive set of instruments has been sent out, and it seems intended that the natural sciences should be studied there, the managers of the present institution take care that their boys should have as little time as possible for such pursuits, by requiring from them all, without exception, a laborious study of Sanskrit, and all the useless, and worse than useless, literature of their ancestors. A good deal of this has been charged (and in some little degree charged with justice) against the exclusive attention paid to Greek and logic, till lately, in Oxford.

But in Oxford we have never been guilty (since a
better system was known in the world at large) of
teaching the physics of Aristotle, however we may
have paid an excessive attention to his metaphysics
and dialectics.

" In Benares, however, I found in the institution supported by Government a professor lec-
turing on astronomy after the system of Ptolemy
and Albunazar, while one of the most forward
boys was at the pains of casting my horoscope;
and the majority of the school were toiling at
Sanskrit grammar. And yet the day before, in
the same holy city, I had visited another college,
founded lately by a wealthy Hindu banker, and
entrusted by him to the management of the
Church Missionary Society, in which, besides a
grammatical knowledge of the Hindusthanee language, as well as Persian and Arabic, the senior
boys could pass a good examination in English
grammar, in Hume's History of England, Joyce's
Scientific Dialogues, the use of the globes, and
the principal facts and moral precepts of the
Gospel, most of them writing beautifully in the
Persian and very tolerably in the English character, and excelling most boys I have met with in
the accuracy and readiness of their arithmetic.
* * * Ram Mohun Roy, a learned native,

who has sometimes been called, though I fear
without reason, a Christian, remonstrated against
this system last year in a paper which he sent me
to be put into Lord Amherst's hands, and which,
for its good English, good sense, and forcible arguments, is a real curiosity, as coming from an
Asiatic. I have not since been in Calcutta, and
know not whether any improvement has occurred
in consequence; but from the unbounded attachment to Sanskrit literature displayed by some of
those who chiefly manage those affairs, I have no
great expectation of the kind. Of the value of
the acquirements which so much is sacrificed to
retain I can only judge from translations, and
they certainly do not seem to me worth picking
out of the rubbish under which they were sink-
ing. Some of the poetry of the Mahabarat I am
told is good, and I think a good deal of the Ra-
mayuna pretty. But no work has yet been produced which even pretends to be authentic history.
No useful discoveries in science are, I believe, so
much as expected; and I have no great sympathy
with those students who value a worthless tract
merely because it calls itself old, or a language
which teaches nothing, for the sake of its copiousness and intricacy. If I were to run wild after
oriental learning I should certainly follow that of

the Mussulmans, whose histories seem really very
much like those of Europe, and whose poetry, so
far as I am yet able to judge, has hardly had justice done to it in the ultra flowery translations
which have appeared in the West."

Bishop Heber's account of his visit to the
Sanskrit college at Benares is strikingly characteristic of the system of public instruction described
in the above extract. It presents a picture which
would be highly amusing, if the mental and moral
darkness which must be the result of such a system
were not calculated to excite feelings of the deepest
melancholy.

"Suttees are less numerous in Benares than
many parts of India, but self-immolation by drown-
ing is very common. Many scores, every year,
of pilgrims from all parts of India come hither
expressly to end their days and secure their sal-
vation. They purchase two large Kedgeree pots,
between which they tie themselves, and when
empty these support their weight in the water.
Thus equipped, they paddle into the stream, then
fill the pots with the water which surrounds them,
and thus sink into eternity. Government have
sometimes attempted to prevent this practice, but
with no other effect than driving the voluntary
victims a little further down the river; nor indeed, when a man has come several hundred miles

to die, is it likely that a police officer can prevent
him.   Instruction seems the only way in which
these poor people can be improved, and that, I
trust, they will by degrees obtain from us.

" The Vidalaya is a large building divided into
two courts, galleried above and below, and full of
teachers and scholars, divided into a number of
classes, who learn reading, writing, arithmetic, (in
the Hindoo manner,) Persian, Hindoo law, and
sacred literature, Sanskrit, astronomy according to
the Ptolemaic system, and astrology !   There are
200 scholars, some of whom of all sorts came to
say their lessons to me, though, unhappily, I was
myself able to profit by none, except the astronomy, and a little of the Persian.   The astrono-
mical lecturer produced a terrestrial globe, divided
according to their system, and elevated to the
meridian of Benares.   Mount Meru he identified
with the north pole, and under the southern pole
he supposed the tortoise "chukwa" to stand, on
which the earth rests.   The southern hemisphere
he apprehended to be uninhabitable, but on its
concave surface, in the interior of the globe, he
placed Padalon.   He then showed me how the
sun went round the earth once in every day, and
how, by a different but equally continuous motion, he also visited the signs of the zodiac.   The
whole system is precisely that of Ptolemy, and

the contrast was very striking between the rubbish which these young men were learning in a
government establishment and the rudiments of
real knowledge which those whom I had visited
the day before had acquired, in the very same
city, and under circumstances far less favourable.
I was informed that it had been frequently proposed to introduce an English and mathematical
class, and to teach the Newtonian and Copernican
system of astronomy; but that the late superintendent of the establishment was strongly opposed to
any innovation, partly on the plea that it would draw
the boys off from their Sanskrit studies, and partly
lest it should interfere with the religious prejudices of the professors. The first of these arguments is pretty much like what was urged at
Oxford (substituting Greek for Sanskrit) against
the new examinations, by which, however, Greek
has lost nothing. The second is plainly absurd,
since the Ptolemaic system, which is now taught,
is itself an innovation, and an improvement on
the old faith of eight worlds and seven oceans,
arranged like a nest of foxes."

My readers may be surprised to hear that this
college had been "completely re-organized*" four

* Education Committee's Report, published in 1831.

years before by Professor Wilson, who went on
deputation to Benares on purpose. But a reform conducted on oriental principles, means
exactly the reverse of what is usually understood
by a reform. In this case, correctness can be obtained only at the expense of increased absurdity;
and the nearer we approach to the standard,
the further we must depart from truth and
reason.

In the passage first quoted, Bishop Heber calls
attention to a paper sent to him by Ram Mohun
Roy to be put into Lord Amherst's hands, " which
for its good English, good sense, and forcible
arguments, is a real curiosity as coming from an
Asiatic." This paper was a remonstrance against
the establishment of the Sanskrit college at Calcutta, which was founded by Lord Amherst, in
imitation of the older institution at Benares, long
after the natives had become awakened to the
value of European instruction, and had instituted
from their own funds, without any assistance from
the government, the Hindu college at Calcutta
and the English school at Benares described by
Bishop Heber, for the purpose of securing for their
children the benefit of such instruction. Ram
Mohun Roy had the improvement of his countrymen sincerely at heart, and he was sufficiently

acquainted both with oriental and European literature to be able to form a correct opinion of
their relative value. His address to Lord Amherst on this occasion deserves the eulogium bestowed on it by Bishop Heber; and as it is quite
to the point, I shall quote it entire.

> " To His Excellency the Right Honourable
> Lord Amherst, Governor General in
> Council.

" My Lord,

" Humbly reluctant as the natives of India are
to obtrude upon the notice of government the
sentiments they entertain on any public measure,
there are circumstances when silence would be
carrying this respectful feeling to culpable excess.
The present rulers of India, coming from a distance of many thousand miles to govern a people
whose language, literature, manners, customs, and
ideas, are almost entirely new and strange to
them, cannot easily become so intimately acquainted with their real circumstances as the
natives of the country are themselves. We should
therefore be guilty of a gross dereliction of duty
to ourselves, and afford our rulers just ground of
complaint at our apathy, did we omit on occasions
of importance like the present to supply them

with such accurate information as might enable
them to devise and adopt measures calculated to
be beneficial to the country, and thus second by
our local knowledge and experience their declared benevolent intentions for its improvements.

" The establishment of a new Sanskrit school in
Calcutta evinces the laudable desire of Government to improve the natives of India by education, — a blessing for which they must ever be
grateful; and every well-wisher of the human race
must be desirous that the efforts made to promote
it should be guided by the most enlightened principles, so that the stream of intelligence may flow
in the most useful channels.

" When this seminary of learning was proposed,
we understood that the government in England
had ordered a considerable sum of money to be
annually devoted to the instruction of its Indian
subjects. We were filled with sanguine hopes
that this sum would be laid out in employing
European gentlemen of talents and education to
instruct the natives of India in mathematics, natural philosophy, chemistry, anatomy, and other
useful sciences, which the nations of Europe have
carried to a degree of perfection that has raised
them above the inhabitants of other parts of the
world.

" While we looked forward with pleasing hope to the dawn of knowledge thus promised to the rising generation, our hearts were filled with mingled feelings of delight and gratitude; we already offered up thanks to Providence for inspiring the most generous and enlightened nations of the West with the glorious ambition of planting in Asia the arts and sciences of modern Europe.

" We find that the government are establishing a Sanskrit school under Hindu pundits, to impart such knowledge as is already current in India. This seminary (similar in character to those which existed in Europe before the time of Lord Bacon) can only be expected to load the minds of youth with grammatical niceties and metaphysical distinctions of little or no practical use to the possessors or to society. The pupils will there acquire what was known two thousand years ago, with the addition of vain and empty subtilties since produced by speculative men, such as is already commonly taught in all parts of India.

" The Sanskrit language, so difficult that almost a lifetime is necessary for its acquisition, is well known to have been for ages a lamentable check on the diffusion of knowledge; and the learning concealed under this almost impervious

veil is far from sufficient to reward the labour of
acquiring it.   But if it were thought necessary to
perpetuate this language for the sake of the portion of valuable information it contains, this might
be much more easily accomplished by other means
than the establishment of a new Sanskrit college;
for there have been always and are now numerous
professors of Sanskrit in the different parts of the
country engaged in teaching this language as well
as the other branches of literature which are to be
the object of the new seminary.   Therefore their
more diligent cultivation, if desirable, would be
effectually promoted by holding out premiums
and granting certain allowances to their most
eminent professors, who have already undertaken
on their own account to teach them, and would
by such rewards be stimulated to still greater
exertions.

" From these considerations, as the sum set
apart for the instruction of the natives of India
was intended by the government in England for
the improvement of its Indian subjects, I beg
leave to state, with due deference to your Lordship's exalted situation, that if the plan now
adopted be followed, it will completely defeat the
object proposed; since no improvement can be
expected from inducing young men to consume a

dozen of years of the most valuable period of their lives in acquiring the niceties of Byakaran or Sanskrit grammar. For instance, in learning to discuss such points as the following: khad, signifying to eat, khaduti, he or she or it eats; query, whether does khaduti, taken as a whole, convey the meaning he, she, or it eats, or are separate parts of this meaning conveyed by distinctions of the word? As if in the English language it were asked, how much meaning is there in the *eat,* how much in the *s?* and is the whole meaning of the word conveyed by these two portions of it distinctly, or by them taken jointly?

" Neither can much improvement arise from such speculations as the following, which are the themes suggested by the Vedant:—in what manner is the soul absorbed into the deity? what relation does it bear to the divine essence? Nor will youths be fitted to be better members of society by the vedantic doctrines, which teach them to believe that all visible things have no real existence; that as father, brother, &c. have no actual entity, they consequently deserve no real affection, and therefore the sooner we escape from them and leave the world the better. Again, no essential benefit can be derived by the student of the Mimangsa from knowing what it is that

makes the killer of a goat sinless on pronouncing
certain passages of the Vedant, and what is the
real nature and operative influence of passages of
the Vedas, &c.

" The student of the Nyayushastra cannot be
said to have improved his mind after he has
learned from it into how many ideal classes the
objects in the universe are divided, and what
speculative relation the soul bears to the body,
the body to the soul, the eye to the ear, &c.

" In order to enable your Lordship to appreciate
the utility of encouraging such imaginary learning
as above characterized, I beg your Lordship will
be pleased to compare the state of science and
literature in Europe before the time of Lord Bacon
with the progress of knowledge made since he
wrote.

" If it had been intended to keep the British
nation in ignorance of real knowledge, the Baconian
philosophy would not have been allowed to dis-
place the system of the schoolmen, which was the
best calculated to perpetuate ignorance. In the
same manner the Sanskrit system of education
would be the best calculated to keep this country
in darkness, if such had been the policy of the
British legislature. But as the improvement of
the native population is the object of the govern-

ment, it will consequently promote a more liberal and enlightened system of instruction ; embracing mathematics, natural philosophy, chemistry, anatomy, with other useful sciences, which may be accomplished with the sum proposed by employing a few gentlemen of talents and learning educated in Europe, and providing a college furnished with necessary books, instruments, and other apparatus.

" In representing this subject to your Lordship I conceive myself discharging a solemn duty which I owe to my countrymen, and also to that enlightened sovereign and legislature which have extended their benevolent care to this distant land, actuated by a desire to improve its inhabitants, and therefore humbly trust you will excuse the liberty I have taken in thus expressing my sentiments to your Lordship.

" I have the honour, &c.

(Signed) " RAM MOHUN ROY."

This memorial was handed over by Lord Amherst to the education committee, and the fate it met with may be conjectured from the spirit which then animated that body. The memorial remained unanswered, and the design of founding a new Sanskrit college was carried into execution.

The opinion entertained on this subject by an

Indian statesman of Sir Charles Metcalfe's established character and long practical experience
cannot fail to be regarded with interest. He
considers Sanskrit and Arabic books as mere
"waste paper," as far as national education is
concerned. His words are, "The government
having resolved to discontinue, with some exceptions, the printing of the projected editions of
oriental works, *a great portion of the limited education fund having hitherto been expended on similar
publications to little purpose but to accumulate stores
of waste paper*, cannot furnish pecuniary aid to the
society for the further printing of those works,
but will gladly make over the parts already
printed either to the Asiatic Society or to any
society or individuals who may be disposed to
complete the publication at their own expense."
The Asiatic Society had applied to the government for funds to complete the printing of the
oriental works which had been discontinued by
the education committee, and this was the answer
which was returned. In another part of this paper,
Sir C. Metcalfe fully admits the valuable and laudable nature of the pursuits in which the Asiatic
Society was engaged, but he uses, as we have
seen, the most emphatic language to express his
sense of the unsuitableness of Arabic and Sanskrit

folios for the enlightenment of the people, and the consequent impropriety of contributing towards the printing of them out of the limited fund which had been set apart for the purpose of national education.

Both Sir Charles Metcalfe and Lord Auckland, who have presided over the administration of India since Lord William Bentinck's departure, have given their full and cordial support to the education committee in carrying into effect the plans of the last-mentioned nobleman. It is not likely that three such men should be mistaken on a point to which, from its important bearing on Indian interests, they must have given a large share of their attention.*

The last authority to which I shall advert is the highest that can be had recourse to on Indian affairs. The Bengal government had reported certain measures adopted by it for the reform of the existing oriental colleges, and the establishment of the new Sanskrit college at Calcutta, and on the 18th February 1821 the court of directors,

* Among other proofs of the sincere interest which the present Governor General takes in the subject, he has built at his own expense a prettily designed schoolhouse in the park at Barrackpoor ; and in this he has established a large English school, which he often visits, to watch the improvement and direct the studies of the pupils.

E

with the sanction of the board of control, replied
as follows:—

" The ends proposed in the institution of the
Hindu* college, and the same
may be affirmed of the Mohammedan, were two: the first,
to make a favourable impression, by our encouragement of
their literature, upon the minds
of the natives; and the second,
to promote useful learning.
You acknowledge, that if the
plan has had any effect of the former kind, it has
had none of the latter; and you add, that ' it
must be feared that the discredit attaching to
such a failure has gone far to destroy the influence
which the liberality of the endowments would
otherwise have had.'

Paras. 230 to 238;
also letter, 10th March
1821, paras. 153 to 180.
State of the Madressa
or Mohammedan col-
lege at Calcutta, and of
the Hindu college at
Benares, with measures
adopted for their im-
provement, and estab-
lishment of a Hindu
college at Calcutta, in
lieu of the proposed
Hindu college at Nud-
dea and Tirhoot.

" We have from time to time been assured, that
these colleges, though they had not till then been
useful, were, in consequence of proposed arrangements, just about to become so; and we have
received from you a similar prediction on the present occasion.

* The new Sanskrit college at Calcutta is meant, as is evident
from the context, and from the abstract in the margin of the
original dispatch.

' We are by no means sanguine in our expectation, that the slight reforms which you have proposed to introduce will be followed by much improvement; and we agree with you in certain doubts, whether a greater degree of activity, even if it were produced on the part of the masters, would, in present circumstances, be attended with the most desirable results.

" With respect to the sciences, it is worse than a waste of time to employ persons either to teach or to learn them in the state in which they are found in the oriental books. As far as any historical documents may be found in the oriental languages, what is desirable is, that they should be translated; and this, it is evident, will best be accomplished by Europeans who have acquired the requisite knowledge. Beyond these branches, what remains in oriental literature is poetry; but it never has been thought necessary to establish colleges for the cultivation of poetry, nor is it certain that this would be the most effectual expedient for the attainment of the end.

" In the meantime, we wish you to be fully apprized of our zeal for the progress and improvement of education among the natives of India, and of our willingness to make considerable sacrifices to that important end, if proper means for

the attainment of it could be pointed out to us;
but we apprehend that the plan of the institutions,
to the improvement of which our attention is now
directed, was originally and fundamentally erroneous. The great end should not have been to
teach Hindu learning or Mohammedan learning,
but useful learning. No doubt, in teaching useful
learning to the Hindus or Mohammedans, Hindu
media or Mohammedan *media*, as far as they were
found the most effectual, would have been proper
to be employed, and Hindu and Mohammedan
prejudices would have needed to be consulted,
while every thing which was useful in Hindu or
Mohammedan literature it would have been proper
to retain; nor would there have been any insu-
perable difficulty in introducing, under these re-
servations, a system of instruction from which
great advantage might have been derived. In
professing, on the other hand, to establish seminaries for the purpose of teaching mere Hindu
or mere Mohammedan literature, you bound your-
selves to teach a great deal of what was frivolous,
not a little of what was purely mischievous, and a
small remainder, indeed, in which utility was in
any way concerned.

" We think that you have taken, upon the
whole, a rational view of what is best to be done.

In the institutions which exist on a particular footing alterations should not be introduced more rapidly than a due regard to existing interests and feelings will dictate; at the same time that incessant endeavours should be used to supersede what is useless or worse in the present course of study by what your better knowledge will recommend.

" In the new college which is to be instituted, and which we think you have acted judiciously in placing at Calcutta, instead of Nuddea and Tirhoot, as originally sanctioned, it will be much further in your power, because not fettered by any preceding practice, to consult the principle of utility in the course of study which you may prescribe. Trusting that the proper degree of attention will be given to this important object, we desire that an account of the plan which you approve may be transmitted to us, and that an opportunity of communicating to you our sentiments upon it may be given to us, before any attempt to carry it into execution is made."

This dispatch was referred to the education committee, who stated in reply, that in proposing the improvement of men's minds it is first necessary to secure their conviction that such improvement is desirable; that tuition in European science

was neither amongst the sensible wants of the
people, nor in the power of the government to
bestow *; that the maulavee and pundit, satisfied
with their own learning, are little inquisitive as to
anything beyond it, and are not disposed to regard
the literature and science of the West as worth the
labour of attainment; and that any attempt to
enforce an acknowledgment of the superiority of
the intellectual productions of the West could
only create dissatisfaction.

This brings us to the second point which we had
to consider, namely, whether, supposing English
literature to be best adapted for the improvement
of the people of India, they are themselves ready
to profit by the advantages which it holds out. If
it can be proved that tuition in European science
has become one of the sensible wants of the people,
and that, so far from being satisfied with their own
learning, they display an eager avidity to avail
themselves of every opportunity of acquiring the
knowledge of the West, it must be admitted that the
case put by the committee of 1824 has occurred,

---

* This letter was dated on the 18th August 1824. The Hindu
college was established in 1816, by the voluntary subscription of
the natives themselves, for the purpose of instructing their youth
in European science, for which no provision had at that time been
made by the government.

and that, according to their own rule, the time has arrived when instruction in western literature and science may be given on an extensive scale, without any fear of producing a reaction.

The proofs that such is the actual state of things have been already touched upon. As the principle of the school book society is, to print only such books as are in demand, and to dispose of them only to those who pay for them, its operations furnish, perhaps, the best test of the existing condition of public feeling in regard to the different systems of learning which are simultaneously cultivated in India. It appears, from their last printed report, that from January 1834 to December 1835 the following sales were effected by them: —

English books - -	31,649
Anglo-Asiatic, or books partly in English and partly in some eastern language - -	4,525
Bengalee - - -	5,754
Hinduee - - - -	4,171
Hindusthanee - - -	3,384
Persian - - -	1,454
Uriya - - - -	834
Arabic - - -	36
Sanskrit - - -	16

E 4

Indeed, books in the learned native languages are such a complete drug in the market that the school book society has for some time past ceased to print them; and that society, as well as the education committee, has a considerable part of its capital locked up in Sanskrit and Arabic lore, which was accumulated during the period when the oriental mania carried every thing before it. Twenty-three thousand such volumes, most of them folios and quartos, filled the library, or rather the lumber room, of the education committee at the time when the printing was put a stop to, and during the preceding three years their sale had not yielded quite one thousand rupees.

At all the oriental colleges, besides being instructed gratuitously, the students had monthly stipends allowed them, which were periodically augmented till they quitted the institution. At the English seminaries, not only was this expedient for obtaining pupils quite superfluous, but the native youth were ready themselves to pay for the privilege of being admitted. The average monthly collection on this account from the pupils of the Hindu college for February and March 1836 was, sicca rupees, 1,325. Can there be more conclusive evidence of the real state of the demand than this? The Hindu college is held under the same roof as the new Sanskrit college, at which thirty pupils were hired at 8 rupees each, and seventy at 5 rupees, or 590 rupees a month in all.

The Hindu college was founded by the voluntary contributions of the natives themselves as early as 1816. In 1831 the committee reported, that "a taste for English had been widely disseminated, and independent schools conducted by young men reared in the Vidyalaya (the Hindu college) are springing up in every direction." * This spirit, gathering strength from time and from many favourable circumstances, had gained a great height in 1835; several rich natives had established English schools at their own expense; associations had been formed for the same purpose at different places in the interior, similar to the one to which the Hindu college owed its origin. The young men who had finished their education propagated a taste for our literature, ano, partly as teachers of benevolent or proprietary schools, partly as tutors in private families, aided all classes in its acquirement. The tide had set in strongly in favour of English education, and when the committee declared itself on the same side, the public support they

* The entire extract will be found at page 8.

received rather went beyond, than fell short of what was required. More applications were received for the establishment of schools than could be complied with; there were more candidates for admission to many of those which were established than could be accommodated. On the opening of the Hoogly college, in August 1836, students of English flocked to it in such numbers as to render the organization and classification of them a matter of difficulty. Twelve hundred names were entered on the books of this department of the college within three days, and at the end of the year there were upwards of one thousand in regular attendance. The Arabic and Persian classes of the institution at the same time mustered less than two hundred. There appears to be no limit to the number of scholars, except that of the number of teachers whom the committee is able to provide. Notwithstanding the extraordinary concourse of English students at Hoogly, the demand was so little exhausted, that when an auxiliary school was lately opened within two miles of the college, the English department of it was instantly filled, and numerous applicants were sent away unsatisfied. In the same way, when additional means of instruction were provided at Dacca, the number of pupils rose at once from

150 to upwards of 300, and more teachers were still called for. The same thing also took place at Agra. These are not symptoms of a forced and premature effort, which, as the committee of 1824 justly observed, would have recoiled upon ourselves, and have retarded our ultimate success.

To sum up what has been said: the Hindu system of learning contains so much truth as to have raised the nation to its present point of civilization, and to have kept it there for ages without retrogading, and so much error as to have prevented it from making any sensible advance during the same long period. Under this system, history is made up of fables, in which the learned in vain endeavour to trace the thread of authentic narrative; its medicine is quackery; its geography and astronomy are monstrous absurdity; its law is composed of loose contradictory maxims, and barbarous and ridiculous penal provisions; its religion is idolatry; its morality is such as might be expected from the example of the gods and the precepts of the religion. Suttee, Thuggee, human sacrifices, Ghaut murder, religious suicides, and other such excrescences of Hinduism, are either expressly enjoined by it, or are directly deduced from the principles inculcated by it. This whole system of sacred and profane learning is knitted and bound together by the sanction of religion; every part of it is an article of faith, and its science is as unchangeable as its divinity. Learning is confined by it to the Brahmins, the high priests of the system, by whom and for whom it was devised. All the other classes are condemned to perpetual ignorance and dependence; their appropriate occupations are assigned by the laws of caste, and limits are fixed, beyond which no personal merit or personal good fortune can raise them. The peculiar wonder of the Hindu system is, not that it contains so much or so little true knowledge, but that it has been so skilfully contrived for arresting the progress of the human mind, as to exhibit it at the end of two thousand years fixed at nearly the precise point at which it was first moulded. The Mohammedan system of learning is many degrees better, and " resembles that which existed among the nations of Europe before the invention of printing;" * so far does even this fall short of the

* These are the words in which Mr. Adam sums up his description of Mohammedan learning in India ; and the real state of the case could not be more accurately described. Gibbon's sketch of Moslem learning will be found in the 52d chapter of the Decline and Fall of the Roman Empire, under the heads, " Their real progress in the sciences," and " Want of erudition, taste, and freedom." But

knowledge with which Europe is now blessed. These are the systems under the influence of which the people of India have become what they are. They have been weighed in the balance, and have been found wanting. To perpetuate them, is to perpetuate the degradation and misery of the people. Our duty is not to teach, but to unteach them, — not to rivet the shackles which have for ages bound down the minds of our subjects, but to allow them to drop off by the lapse of time and the progress of events.

If we turn from Sanskrit and Arabic learning, and the state of society which has been formed by it, to western learning, and the improved and still rapidly improving condition of the western nations, what a different spectacle presents itself! Through the medium of England, India has been brought into the most intimate connection with this fa-

---

however defective Arabian learning may appear when viewed by the light of modern science, it would be doing great injustice to the Augustan age of the caliphs at Bagdad to compare it with the present æra of Mohammedan literature in India. The Indian Mohammedans are only bad imitators of an erroneous system. Arabic is studied at Calcutta as a difficult foreign language ; original genius and research have long since died out, if they ever had any existence, among this class of literary people in India ; and the astronomy of Ptolemy and the medicine of Galen are languidly transmitted by the dogmatic teachers of one generation to the patient disciples of the next.

voured quarter of the globe, and the particular
claims of the English language as an instrument
of Indian improvement have thus become a point
of paramount importance. These claims have
been thus described by one who will be admitted
to have made good his title to an opinion on the
subject :—

" How then stands the case? We have to educate a people who cannot at present be educated
by means of their mother tongue; we must teach
them some foreign language. The claims of our
own language it is hardly necessary to recapi-
tulate; it stands pre-eminent even among the
languages of the West; it abounds with works of
imagination not inferior to the noblest which
Greece has bequeathed to us; with models of
every species of eloquence; with historical compositions which, considered merely as narratives
have seldom been surpassed, and which, considered as vehicles of ethical and political instruction, have never been equalled; with just
and lively representations of human life and
human nature; with the most profound speculations on metaphysics, morals, government, jurisprudence, trade; with full and correct information respecting every experimental science which
tends to preserve the health, to increase the com-

fort, or to expand the intellect of man. Whoever knows that language has ready access to all the vast intellectual wealth which all the wisest nations of the earth have created and hoarded in the course of ninety generations. It may safely be said that the literature now extant in that language is of far greater value than all the literature which three hundred years ago was extant in all the languages of the world together. Nor is this all: in India English is the language spoken by the ruling class; it is spoken by the higher class of natives at the seats of government; it is likely to become the language of commerce throughout the seas of the East; it is the language of two great European communities which are rising, the one in the south of Africa, the other in Austral-Asia, — communities which are every year becoming more important and more closely connected with our Indian Empire. Whether we look at the intrinsic value of our literature, or at the particular situation of this country, we shall see the strongest reason to think that, of all foreign tongues, the English tongue is that which would be the most useful to our native subjects."

As of all existing languages and literatures the English is the most replete with benefit to the

human race, so it is overspreading the earth with
a rapidity far exceeding any other. With a partial
exception in Canada, English is the language of
the continent of America north of Mexico; and
at the existing rate of increase there will be a
hundred millions of people speaking English in
the United States alone at the end of this century.
In the West India islands we have given our
language to a population collected from various
parts of Africa, and by this circumstance alone
they have been brought many centuries nearer to
civilization than their countrymen in Africa, who
may for ages grope about in the dark, destitute of
any means of acquiring true religion and science.
Their dialect is an uncouth perversion of English
suited to the present crude state of their ideas,
but their literature will be the literature of England, and their language will gradually be conformed
to the same standard. More recently the English
language has taken root in the continent of Africa
itself, and a nation is being formed by means of
it in the extensive territory belonging to the Cape
out of a most curious mixture of different races.
But the scene of its greatest triumphs will be in
Asia. To the south a new continent is being
peopled with the English race; to the north, an

ancient people, who have always taken the lead in the progress of religion and science in the east,* have adopted the English language as their language of education, by means of which they are becoming animated by a new spirit, and are entering at once upon the improved knowledge of Europe, the fruit of the labour and invention of successive ages. The English language, not many generations hence, will be spoken by millions in all the four quarters of the globe; and our learning, our morals, our principles of constitutional liberty, and our religion, embodied in the established literature, and diffused through the genius of the vernacular languages, will spread far and wide among the nations.

The objection, therefore, to the early proceedings of the education committee is, that they were calculated to produce a revival, not of sound learning, but of antiquated and pernicious errors.

* The Buddhist religion, which originated in Behar, has spread to the furthest extremity of China, and the intervening nations have always been accustomed to regard India as the fountain-head both of learning and religion. Thibetan literature is a translation from Sanskrit, and the vernacular language of Behar is the sacred language of Burmah and the adjoining countries. It may be hoped that India will hereafter become the centre of a purer faith. The innumerable islands of the South must also be powerfully acted upon by Austral-Asia, which has been wonderfully reserved to be erected at once into a civilized and powerful country in the darkest region of eastern barbarism.

The pupils in the oriental seminaries were trained in a complete course of Arabic and Sanskrit learning, including the theology of the Vedas and the Koran, and were turned out accomplished maulavees and pundits,—the very class whom the same committee described as "satisfied with their own learning, little inquisitive as to any thing beyond it, and not disposed to regard the literature and science of the West as worth the labour of attainment." And having been thus educated, they were sent to every part of the country to fill the most important situations which were open to the natives, the few who could not be provided for in this way taking service as private tutors or family priests. Every literary attempt connected with the old learning at the same time received the most liberal patronage, and the country was deluged with Arabic and Sanskrit books. By acting thus, the committee created the very evil which they professed to fear. They established great corporations, with ramifications in every district, the feelings and interest of whose members were deeply engaged on the side of the prevailing errors. All the murmuring which has been heard has come from this quarter; all the opposition which has been experienced has been headed by persons supported by our stipends, and trained in our colleges. The money spent on the Arabic and Sanskrit colleges was, therefore, not merely a dead loss to the cause of truth; it was bounty money paid to raise up champions of error, and to call into being an oriental interest which was bound by the condition of its existence to stand in the front of the battle against the progress of European literature.

In the five districts named in the margin, one of which contains the former Moham- Murshedabad, medan capital of Bengal, Mr. Adam Bheerbhoom, Burdwan, found only 158 students of Arabic South Behar, Tirhoot. learning. In the single government college of Calcutta there are 114 students. Although supported and patronised by the British government, this college differs in no respect from the Mohammedan colleges at Constantinople and Bokhara. It is as completely a seminary of genuine unmitigated Mohammedanism as the Jesuits' college at Rome is a seminary of Roman catholicism. It is considered by the Moslems as the head quarters of their religion in Bengal, and it has made Calcutta the radiating centre, not of civilization, as it ought only to be, but, to a lamentable extent, of bigotry and error.

The Sanskrit college was a still more desperate

attempt to reproduce the feelings and habits of thought of past ages in the midst of a comparatively enlightened community. By establishing the Hindu college at their own expense, the Hindus had seven years before given a decisive proof that it was instruction in English and not in Sanskrit which they required. But, in spite of this evidence, the act with which we signalised the commencement of our educational operations was the establishment of a Brahminical college, in which false science and false religion are systematically taught, in which the priestly domination and monopoly of learning are maintained both by practice * and precept, and the members of which, although they reside at the head quarters of British Indian civilization, are always present in spirit with the founders of the Hindu system, with whom they daily converse, and to whose age they really belong. Can we wonder that the young men educated at such a seminary are, according to their own confession, burdens to the public, and objects of contempt to their countrymen? It might have succeeded if it had been established a thousand years ago; but the institu-

* None but Brahmins and a few persons of the medical caste are admitted to study at this institution.

tions of a barbarous age will not satisfy a people whose eyes have been opened, and who are craving after true knowledge.

After the committee had confessed that " a taste for English had been widely disseminated, and independent schools, conducted by young men reared in the Hindu college, were springing up in every direction *," it might have been expected that they would have modified their plan of proceeding. It was admitted, that to give instruction in European science was their ultimate object; it also appears from their report that this was the only part of their operations which was propagating itself, and proceeding with an independent spring of action; why, therefore, was scope not given to it?

For some time after this, however, we continued to prop up barbarism by the power of civilization, and to avail ourselves of the enormous influence of the English government to press on the people decayed and noxious systems, which they themselves rejected. That we did not succeed in giving to those systems a more effectual impulse was not owing to any want of exertion on our

---

* See the whole extract at page 8.

part. We pushed them as far or farther than they would go, and it was only because the natives would not buy the books printed by us, or read them without being paid to do so, that a change was at last resolved on.

CHAP. IV.

Objections answered. — Construction of the Charter Act of 1813. — Change in the Employment of the public Endowments for the Encouragement of Learning. — Abolition of Stipends. — Probability of the Natives being able to prosecute the Study of English with effect.— The alleged Necessity of cultivating Arabic and Sanskrit for the sake of improving the vernacular Languages. — The Plan of employing Maulavees and Pundits as our Agents for the Propagation of European Science.— Whether or not it is our Duty to patronise the same Kind of Learning as our Predecessors.

I SHALL now proceed to reply, with as much brevity as circumstances will admit, to the objections which have been urged to the change in the committee's plan of operation made in accordance with the resolution of the Indian government, dated the 7th March 1835; and as my object is not to write a book of my own, but to put this important subject, once for all, in a clear point of view, I shall continue to avail myself of the writings of others whenever they express what I have to say better than I could express it myself.

The heads of objection will be taken from an article by Professor Wilson, entitled " Education of the Natives of India," published in the Asiatic Journal for January 1836, which contains the most complete statement which has yet appeared of all that can be said on the oriental side of the question.

The first in order relates to the construction of that part of the charter act of 1813 by which a lac of rupees a year was assigned for the education of the natives of India. The opponents of our present plan of proceeding contend that it was not the intention of parliament, in making this assignment, to encourage the cultivation of sound learning and true principles of science, but to bring about a revival of the antiquated and false learning of the shasters, which had fallen into neglect in consequence of the cessation of the patronage which had in ancient times been extended to it by the native Hindu princes. To this argument the following reply has been made :—

" It does not appear to me that the act of parliament can by any art of construction be made to bear the meaning which has been assigned to it. It contains nothing about the particular languages or sciences which are to be studied. A

sum is set apart 'for the revival and promotion
of literature, and the encouragement of the
learned natives of India, and for the introduction
and promotion of a knowledge of the sciences
among the inhabitants of the British territories.'
It is argued, or rather taken for granted, that by
literature the parliament can have meant only
Arabic and Sanskrit literature; that they never
would have given the honourable appellation of a
'learned native' to a native who was familiar with
the poetry of Milton, the metaphysics of Locke,
and the physics of Newton; but that they meant
to designate by that name only such persons as
might have studied in the sacred books of the
Hindus all the uses of Cusa-grass, and all the
mysteries of absorption into the deity. This does
not appear to be a very satisfactory interpretation.
To take a parallel case: suppose that the pacha of
Egypt, a country once superior in knowledge to
the nations of Europe, but now sunk far below
them, were to appropriate a sum for the purpose
of 'reviving and promoting literature, and encouraging learned natives of Egypt,' would anybody
infer that he meant the youth of his pachalic to
give years to the study of hieroglyphics, to search
into all the doctrines disguised under the fable of
Osiris, and to ascertain with all possible accuracy

F

the ritual with which cats and onions were anciently adored? Would he be justly charged with inconsistency if, instead of employing his young subjects in deciphering obelisks, he were to order them to be instructed in the English and French languages, and in all the sciences to which those languages are the chief keys?

" The words on which the supporters of the old system rely do not bear them out, and other words follow which seem to be quite decisive on the other side. This lac of rupees is set apart, not only for ' reviving literature in India,' the phrase on which their whole interpretation is founded, but also ' for the introduction and promotion of a knowledge of the sciences among the inhabitants of the British territories,'—words which are alone sufficient to authorize all the changes for which I contend."

Both the court of directors and the Indian government took this view of the subject at the period when measures were first taken to carry the intentions of the British parliament into effect, and those intentions were certainly likely to have been better understood at that time than at any subsequent period. The Indian government in their instructions to the committee appointed to administer the funds made no allusion to the supposed necessity for reviving oriental literature. On the contrary, they stated the objects for which the committee had been appointed to be "the better instruction of the people, the introduction of useful knowledge, including the arts and sciences of Europe, and the improvement of their moral character," objects with which the learning of the shasters and the Koran, which it was afterwards proposed to revive, are at complete variance. The court of directors in their dispatch written about the same period are still more explicit. They emphatically state that "it is worse than a waste of time to employ persons either to teach or to learn the sciences in the state in which they are found in oriental books;" that "the great end should not have been to teach Hindu learning or Mohammedan learning, but useful learning;" and that, in establishing seminaries for the purpose of teaching mere Hindu or mere Mohammedan literature, the Indian government bound themselves "to teach a great deal of what was frivolous, not a little of what was purely mischievous, and a small remainder indeed in which utility was in any way concerned." But meanwhile the administration of the fund had fallen into the hands of persons devoted to oriental studies, party zeal was excited,

and the ingenuity of several able men was tasked
to the utmost to defend a course of proceeding
which had been adopted in spite of the declared
sentiments of the court of directors and of common sense.

It was urged, in the next place, that it was
downright spoliation to alter the appropriation of
any of the funds which had previously been spent
by the government in encouraging the study of
Sanskrit and Arabic, but which were now directed to be employed in teaching English under the
restrictions contained in the resolution of the
7th March 1835. To this it was replied that
" the grants which are made from the public
purse for the encouragement of literature differ in
no respect from the grants which are made from
the same purse for other objects of real or supposed utility. We found a sanatarium on a spot
which we suppose to be healthy: do we thereby
pledge ourselves to keep a sanatarium there, if the
result should not answer our expectations? We
commence the erection of a pier: is it a violation
of the public faith to stop the work, if we afterwards see reason to believe that the building will
be useless? The rights of property are undoubtedly sacred; but nothing endangers those rights
so much as the practice, now unhappily too com-

mon, of attributing them to things to which they do not belong. Those who would impart to abuses the sanctity of property are in truth imparting to the institution of property the unpopularity and the fragility of abuses. If the government has given to any person a formal assurance,—nay, if the government has excited in any person's mind a reasonable expectation,—that he shall receive a certain income as a teacher or a learner of Sanskrit or Arabic, I would respect that person's pecuniary interests. I would rather err on the side of liberality to individuals than suffer the public faith to be called in question. But to talk of a government pledging itself to teach certain languages and certain sciences, though those languages may become useless, though those sciences may be exploded, seems to me quite unmeaning. There is not a single word in any public instrument from which it can be inferred that the Indian government ever intended to give any pledge on this subject, or ever considered the destination of these funds as unalterably fixed. But, had it been otherwise, I should have denied the competence of our predecessors to bind us by any pledge on such a subject. Suppose that a government had in the last century enacted, in the most solemn manner, that all its subjects should to the

end of time be inoculated for the small-pox; would
that goverment be bound to persist in the practice after Jenner's discovery? These promises,
of which nobody claims the performance, and from
which nobody can grant a release; these vested
rights which vest in nobody; this property without proprietors; this robbery which makes nobody
poorer, — may be comprehended by persons of
higher faculties than mine. I consider this plea
merely as a set form of words, regularly used both
in England and in India in defence of every abuse
for which no other plea can be set up." All the private endowments which have at different times been
placed under the management of the education
committee are administered with a strict regard
to the intentions of the founders. A large sum of
money, for instance, left by a late minister of the
king of Lucknow, which was originally appropriated to the use of the oriental college at Delhi,
continues to be applied to the support of oriental
literature in that institution.

Another objection which has been made is, that
the abolition of the stipends formerly given to
students will exclude the sons of learned men who
are in indigent circumstances, as well as those of
all persons living at a distance from the government colleges, the advantages of which will thus

be confined to the capital and to one or two great towns.

To this I answer, that, instead of two or three, there are already forty institutions scattered throughout the country; that the means of obtaining a liberal education have thus been brought into everybody's own neighbourhood; and that the number of young men belonging to every class of society, and to every part of the Bengal provinces, who now profit by our seminaries, necessarily greatly exceeds what used to be the case under the plan of having a few expensive colleges at which the students as well as teachers received salaries. Hundreds of boys are now cultivating our literature in Assam, Arrakan, Tenasserim, and other frontier provinces, which did not send a single student to the colleges at Calcutta and Benares.

In India poverty is not the only obstacle to the education of children at a distance from their parents. The means of communication from place to place are slow and inconvenient; a journey of one or two hundred miles appears to a native the same formidable undertaking that it did to our ancestors in the time of Queen Elizabeth; and, above all, the mutual confidence which leads Englishmen to trust the entire management of their

children to persons whom they often know only
by reputation, is at a very low ebb in India.   No
native who could afford to give his son an education of any sort at home would think of sending
him to be brought up among strangers.   It was
once proposed to educate the public wards at Calcutta, where the government itself would have
had proper care taken of them, but the relations
of the wards so unanimously and decidedly ob-
jected to the plan that it was at once abandoned.
They had no objection, however, to their being
educated under the superintendence of the government officers at their own provincial towns,
with which they are in almost daily communication, and at which the young men might have
resided, often in their own town houses, under
the care of the old servants of the family.   Besides this, the colleges under the stipendiary system were regarded by all classes as charitable
institutions; and this alone would have prevented
the native gentry from sending their sons to them.
They were filled with the children of indigent
persons, a very small proportion of whom came
from a distance; and these last, even if they had
learned any thing worth communicating, which
they did not, would have been too few, too unin-
fluential, and too much isolated from the rest of

the community, to be able to induce the body of
their countrymen to participate in their opinions.
The animating and civilizing influence arising
from the neighbourhood of a large seminary, and
the daily intercourse of the people with its numerous scholars, and the tendency which this has
to interest the public in the subject of education,
and to lead to the establishment of new institutions, was too partial under the stipendiary system
to have any practical effect. Even if the education
given had been of a kind calculated to enlighten
the people, instead of confirming them in their
errors, it would have taken ages to make an impression on the immense population of western
India by such means as these.

If any class of persons be favoured by the plan
which has now been adopted, it is those who are
able and willing to learn, and who are in a situation to induce others to follow their example.
If any be excluded, it is those who used to come
to obtain food, not for the mind, but for the body,
and who were too poor to be able to pursue their
studies in after life. So long as we offer instruction only, we may be sure that none but willing
students will attend; but if we offer money in
addition to instruction, it becomes impossible to

say for the sake of which they attend. These
bounties on learning are the worst of bounties;
they draw to a particular line a greater number
of persons than that line would, without artificial
encouragement, attract, or than the state of society
requires. They also paralyze exertion. A person
who does not want to learn a particular language
or science is tempted to commence the study by
the stipend; as soon as he has got the stipend
he has no motive for zealously prosecuting the
study. Sluggishness, mediocrity, absence of spi-
rited exertion, and resistance to all improvement
are the natural growth of this system.

It is also of particular importance in such a
country as India, and on such a subject as popular
education, that the government should have some
certain test of the wishes of its subjects. As long
as stipends were allowed, students would of course
have been forthcoming. Now the people must
decide for themselves. Every facility is given, but
no bribes; and if more avail themselves of one
kind of instruction than of another, we may be
sure that it is because such is the real bent of the
public mind. But for the abolition of stipends,
false systems might have been persevered in from
generation to generation, which, with an appear-

ance of popularity, would really have been preserved from falling into disuse only by the patronage of government.

The result of the experiment has been most
satisfactory. Formerly we kept needy boys in
pay, to train them up to be bigoted maulavees
and pundits; now multitudes of the upper and
middle classes flock to our seminaries to learn,
without fee or reward, all that English literature
can teach them. The practice of giving stipends
to students was part of the general system by
which learning was confined to particular castes;
this monopoly has now been broken down, and
all are invited to attend who are really anxious to
learn. Where formerly we paid both teachers
and students, we now only pay the teachers; and
our means of extending our operations have been
proportionably increased; yet, so great is the demand for teachers, that if we could only increase
their number at will, we might have almost any
number of students.

It is constantly urged by the advocates of
oriental learning that the result of all our efforts
will only be to extend a smattering of English
throughout India, and that the question is between a profound knowledge of Sanskrit and
Arabic literature on the one side, and a super-

ficial knowledge of the rudiments of English on the other.

Nothing can be more groundless than this assumption. The medical pupils who were declared by Mr. Prinsep to have passed as good an examination for the time they had attended lectures as any class of pupils in Europe, acquired their knowledge entirely from English books and lectures delivered in English. Neither were these picked boys; they principally came from Mr. Hare's preparatory school, and from the second and third classes of the Hindu college, and they were therefore below the standard of those who go through the whole course of instruction at our principal seminaries.

In their report published in 1831 the committee, speaking of the Hindu college, observe: "The consequence has surpassed expectation; a command of the English language and a familiarity with its literature and science have been acquired to an extent rarely equalled by any schools in Europe." * Such having been the result at the Hindu college, what is there to prevent our being equally successful in the more recently established seminaries? The same class

* The whole extract will be found at page 8.

of youth have to be instructed; the same desire exists on the part of the committee to give them a really good education; we have the same means at our disposal for accomplishing that object. A single show institution at the capital, to be always exhibited and appealed to as a proof of their zeal in the cause of liberal education, might answer very well, as far as the committee themselves are concerned; but what are the people of the interior to do, to whom this education would be equally useful, and who are equally capable of profiting by it? For their sake the committee have now established many Hindu colleges.

English is a much easier language than either Arabic or Sanskrit. " The study of Sanskrit grammar," Mr. Adam observes, " occupies about seven years, lexicology about two, literature about ten, law about ten, logic about thirteen, and mythology about four." The course of study fixed for the Sanskrit college at Calcutta by Professor Wilson embraces twelve years, the first six of which are spent in learning grammar and composition; besides which, the boys are expected to know something of grammar before they are admitted. In three years boys of ordinary abilities get such a command of the English language as to be able to acquire every sort of information by means of it. The Sanskrit is altogether a dead language. The Arabic is not spoken in India. The English is both a living and a spoken language.* The Brahminical and Moslem systems belong to bygone days; a large portion of them has become obsolete; a still larger is only faintly reflected in the habits of the people. The associations connected with the new learning, on the other hand, are gaining ground every day. The English government is established; English principles and institutions are becoming familiarized. to the native mind; English words are extensively adopted into the native languages; teachers, books, and schools are rapidly multiplied; the improvements in the art of education, the result of the extraordinary degree of attention which the subject has received of late years in England, are all applied to facilitate the study of English in India. Infant schools, which have lately been introduced, will enable native children to acquire our language, without any loss of time, as they learn to speak. Nine years ago, when the first English

---

* The familiar use of a living language is an advantage which the teachers of Latin and Greek, as well as those of Sanskrit and Arabic, might envy.

class was established in the upper provinces*, a
few old fashioned English spelling books were with
difficulty procured from the neighbouring stations.
Nine years hence it is probable that an English
education will be every where more cheaply and
easily obtained than an Arabic or Sanskrit one.
It is an error to anticipate the march of events,
but it is not less so to neglect to watch their progress, and to be perpetually judging the existing
state of things by a standard which is applicable
only to past times. " This, too, will acquire the
authority of time; and what we now defend by precedents will itself be reckoned among precedents."

Native children seem to have their faculties
developed sooner, and to be quicker and more
self-possessed than English children. Even when
the language of instruction is English, the English
have no advantage over their native class-fellows.
As far as capability of acquiring knowledge is
concerned, the native mind leaves nothing to be
desired. The faculty of learning languages is
particularly powerful in it. It is unusual to find,
even in the literary circles of the Continent,
foreigners who can express themselves in English
with so much fluency and correctness as we find
in hundreds of the rising generation of Hindus.

* At Delhi.

Readiness in acquiring languages, which exists in such a strong degree in children, seems to exist also in nations which are still rising to manhood. No people speak foreign languages like the Russians and Hindus. Such nations are going through a course of imitation, and those qualities of mind upon which their success depends seem to be proportionably developed.

When we go beyond this point to the higher and more original powers of the mind, judgment, reflection, and invention, it is not so easy to pronounce an opinion. It has been said, that native youth fall behind at the age at which these faculties begin most to develope themselves in Englishmen. But this is the age when the young Englishman generally commences another and far more valuable education, consisting in the preparation for, and practice of some profession requiring severe application of mind; when he has the highest honours and emoluments opened to his view as the reward of his exertions, and when he begins to profit by his daily intercourse with a cultivated intellectual, and moral society. Instead of this, the native youth falls back on the ignorant and depraved mass of his countrymen ; and, till lately, so far from being stimulated to further efforts, he was obliged to ask himself for

what end he had hitherto laboured. Every avenue
to distinction was shut against him; and his acquirements served only to manifest the full extent of his
degraded position. The best test of what they
can do, is what they have done. Their ponderous
and elaborate grammatical systems, their wonderfully subtle metaphysical disquisitions, show them
to have a German perseverance and Greek acuteness; and they certainly have not failed in poetical
composition. What may we not expect from these
powers of mind, invigorated by the cultivation of
true science, and directed towards worthy objects!
The English, like the Hindus, once wasted their
strength on the recondite parts of school learning
All that we can say with certainty is, that the
Hindus are excellent students, and have learned
well up to the point to which their instructors
have as yet conducted them. A new career is now
opened to them: the stores of European knowledge have been placed at their disposal: a cultivated society of their own is growing up: their
activity is stimulated by the prospect of honourable
and lucrative employment. It will be seen what
the next fifty years will bring forth.

To return to the point from which I have di-
gressed; it is true, that a smattering of English
formerly prevailed to a considerable extent, without

any beneficial result; and that English acquirements were held in great contempt. The government then encouraged nothing but Oriental
learning; and English, instead of being cultivated as a literary and scientific language, was
abandoned to menial servants and dependents, who
hoped by means of it to make a profit of the ignorance of their masters. It was first rescued from
this state of degradation by Lord William Bentinck
who made it the language of diplomatic correspondence. * It was afterwards publicly recognised as
the most convenient channel, through which the
upper and middle classes of the natives could obtain access to the knowledge of the West; and
many very good seminaries were established, to
enable them to acquire it. The prejudice against
English has now disappeared, and to know it, has
become a distinction to which people of all classes
aspire. There can be no doubt therefore of our now
being able to make a deep and permanent impression on the Hindu nation through this medium,
if sufficient means of instruction are provided.

Another argument urged for teaching Arabic and
Sanskrit is, that they are absolutely necessary for

* Translations are sent, with the Governor-General's letters, to
the native princes, when there is any doubt as to their being understood.

the improvement of the vernacular dialects. The latter, it is said, are utterly incapable of representing European ideas; and the natives must therefore have recourse to the congenial, accessible, and inexhaustible stores of their classical languages. To adopt English phraseology would be grotesque patchwork; and the condemnation of the classical languages to oblivion, would consign the dialects to utter helplessness and irretrievable barbarism.

The experience both of the East and West demonstrates, that the difficulty which this argument supposes never can exist. If the national language can easily express any new idea which is introduced from abroad, a native term is usually adopted. But, if not, the word, as well as the meaning, are imported together from the same fountain of supply. This is the ordinary process; but the supply of words is not always limited to the strict measure of our wants. Languages are amplified and refined by scholars, who naturally introduce the foreign words with which their minds are charged, and which, from their being in the habit of using them, appear to them to be more expressive than any other. Hence that wealth of words, that choice of verbal signs,—some of domestic and others of foreign origin; some borrowed from cognate, and others from radically different sources,—which characterises the languages of the modern civilised nations. The naturalisation of foreign knowledge is, no doubt, a task of some difficulty; but history proves that as fast as it can be introduced, words are found in more than sufficient abundance to explain it to the people, without any special provision being necessary for that purpose. The greater effort involves the less; and this is the first time any body ever thought of separating them.

Take our own language as an example. Saxon is the ground-work of it; Norman-French was first largely infused into it : then Latin and Greek, on the revival of letters; and, last of all, a few words from other modern languages. Each of these has blended harmoniously with the rest; and the whole together has become one of the most powerful, precise, and copious languages in the world. Yet Latin, and Greek, and French are only very distantly related to the Saxon. It is curious that our own language, which we know to be so consistent and harmonious, had formerly the same reproach of incongruity cast on it. Klopstock called it an ignoble and barbarous mixture of jarring materials; to which Schlegel justly replied, that although English is compounded of different languages, they have been completely fused into one

and that no Englishman ordinarily thinks of the
pedigree of the words which he uses, or is in the
least offended by the difference in their origin.
The same may be said, more or less, of all the
modern European languages. If Bengalee and
Hindusthanee ever become as well fitted for every
purpose of literature and science as English and
French, no person will have reason to complain of
the process by which this may have been effected.

A similar process has been gone through in
India. Sanskrit itself was engrafted by a race of
conquerors on the national languages, and very evident traces of its incongruity with them exist in the
south of India*, and in various hilly tracts. The
Mahommedan invaders afterwards introduced a
profusion of Arabic and Persian, and a few Turk-
ish words. The Portuguese contributed the naval
vocabulary and many other words, which are now
so blended with the vernacular dialects as not to be
distinguishable by the natives from words of ancient
Indian origin. And, lastly, numerous English
words have been already naturalised, and others
are daily becoming so through the medium of our
civil and military systems, of our national customs

---

* The languages of the Peninsula, south of the districts in
which Mahratta is commonly spoken, derive more than half their
words from sources entirely independent of the Sanskrit.

and institutions, and, above all, of our literature and science, which are now extensively cultivated by the rising generation. Of these auxiliary languages, the ancient unadulterated Persian is closely allied to the Sanskrit; but Arabic, with which Persian has been completely saturated since the conquest of Persia by the Arabians*, is as unlike Sanskrit as it is possible for one language to be unlike another. The Sanskrit delights in compounds: the Arabic abhors the composition of words, and expresses complex ideas by circumlocution. The Sanskrit verbal roots are almost universally biliteral: the Arabic roots are as universally triliteral. They have scarcely a single word in common. They are written in opposite directions;—Sanskrit, from left to right; Arabic, from right to left. " In whatever light we view them," observes Sir William Jones, " they seem totally distinct ; and must have been invented by two different races of men." Portuguese and English, on the other hand, through their close connection

---

* Arabic has been extensively introduced into the Indian vernacular languages, both mediately through Persian and immediately from Arabic literature. The complete union of the Arabic with the ancient Persian language, is as much a proof that the most uncongenial languages will readily amalgamate as its union with the Indian dialects.

with Latin and Greek, have a great deal in common with Sanskrit.

In the face of these facts it is gravely asserted to be "indispensably necessary"* to cultivate congenial classical languages, in order to enrich and embellish the popular Indian dialects. Then, with a strange inconsistency, it is proposed to cultivate, for this purpose, as being a congenial language, the Arabic, which is the most radically different from the Indian dialects of any language that could be named; and, lastly, the English language, which has a distant affinity to those dialects, through the Saxon, and a very near connection with them through the Latin and Greek, is rejected as uncongenial.

When we once go beyond the limits of the popular vocabulary, Sanskrit, Arabic, and English are equally new to the people. They have a word to learn which they did not know before; and it is

---

* If the supposed necessity really existed, our language must have been first improved by the cultivation of Anglo-Saxon philology, instead of Norman-French; the fathers of English literature must have coined words from the Teutonic dialects, to express the thoughts of the Greek, Roman, and Italian authors; our vocabularies of war, cookery, and dress-making, instead of being unaltered French, must first have been filtered through a German medium; and in India, every idea which has been adopted from the religion, the learning, and the jurisprudence of the Arabians, must have been translated into good Sanskrit before it could have been naturalised.

as easy for them to learn an English as a Sanskrit word.   Numerous Arabic, English, and Portuguese terms have thus become household words in India, the Sanskrit synonymes of which are utterly unknown to the people.   The first form part and parcel of the popular language: the last have no existence beyond the Shasters and the memories of a few hundred Pundits who are conversant with those old records. A gentleman, holding office in India, lately attempted to reduce to practice the theory now under consideration.   In his official communications to the neighbouring courts, every word not of Sanskrit origin was carefully expunged, and a pure Sanskrit word was substituted for it.   Thus *Sungrahuk* was thrust in the place of *Collector, Sunkhuk* of *Number, Adhesh* of *Hukm, Bhoomadhikaree* of *Zemeendar ;* and so on. The consequence was, that his communications were unintelligible to the persons to whom they were addressed ; and it would have been better if they had been in Persian, from which we had at that time just escaped, than in such a learned jargon.

As it is therefore a matter of indifference from what source the vocabulary is derived, while it is admitted that English must be cultivated for the sake of the knowledge which it contains, will it not be advisable to make English serve both these purposes; to draw upon it for words as well as ideas; to concentrate the national energies on this single point? Otherwise it will be necessary for the same persons to make themselves good English scholars, in order that they may learn chemistry, geology, or mechanics; and good Sanskrit scholars, in order that they may get names to apply to what they have learned. Our main object is, to raise up a class of persons who will make the learning of Europe intelligible to the people of Asia in their own languages. An enlarged and accurate knowledge of the systems they will have to explain, such as can be derived only from a long course of study, will, at any rate, be necessary to qualify them for this important task. But, if they will then have to begin again, and to devote nine years more to the study of Sanskrit philology, we might as well at once abandon the attempt. Neither would it be possible for one set of persons to provide learning, and another words; and for every lecturer or writer on European subjects always to have his philologer at his elbow, to supply him with Sanskrit terms as they are required. Until the duration of human life is doubled, and means are found to maintain the literary class through twice the longest period now allotted to education, such complicated and cumbrous schemes of national improvement will be impracticable: and even if they were practicable, they would be useless. When the people have to learn a new word, it is of no consequence whether they learn at Sanskrit or an English one; and all the time spent in learning Sanskrit would therefore be downright waste.

After a language has once assumed a fixed character, the unnecessary introduction of new words is, no doubt, offensive to good taste. But in Bengalee and Hindusthanee nothing is fixed; every thing is yet to be done, and a new literature has to be formed, almost from the very foundation. The established associations, which are liable to be outraged by the obtrusion of strange words, have therefore no existence in this case. Such refinement is the last stage in the progress of improvement. It is the very luxury of language; and to speak of the delicate sensibility of a Bengalee or Hindusthanee being offended by the introduction of new words to express new ideas, is to transfer to a poor and unformed tongue the feelings which are connected only with a rich and cultivated one. It will be time enough after their scientific vocabulary is settled, and they have masterpieces of their own, to think of keeping their language pure. When they have a native

Milton or Shakspeare, they will not require us to guide them in this respect.

All we have to do is to impregnate the national mind with knowledge. The first depositaries of this knowledge will have a strong personal interest in making themselves intelligible. They will speak to, and write for, their countrymen, with whose habits of mind and extent of information they will be far better acquainted than it is possible for us to be. They will be able to meet each case as it arises far more effectually than it can be done by laying down general rules before-hand. Those who write for the educated classes will freely avail themselves of English scientific terms. Those who write for the people will seek out popular explanations of many of those terms at a sacrifice of precision and accuracy. By degrees, some will drop out of use, while others will retain their place in the national language. Our own language went through this process. After a profuse and often pedantic use of Latin and Greek words by our earlier writers, our vocabulary settled down nearly in its present form, being composed of words partly of indigenous, and partly of foreign, origin, to which occasional additions are still made, as they are required, from both sources. The only safe general rule which can be laid down

on this subject, is to use the word which happens
at the time to be the most intelligible, from whatever language it may be derived, and to leave it to
be determined by experience whether that or some
other ought to be finally adopted.

If English is to be the language of education in
India, it follows, as a matter of course, that it will
be the scientific language also, and that terms will
be borrowed from it to express those ideas for which
no appropriate symbols exist in the popular dialects. The educated class, through whom European knowledge will reach the people, will be
familiar with English. They will adopt the English words with which they are already acquainted, and will be clear gainers by it, while
others will not be losers. The introduction of
English words into the vernacular dialects will
gradually diminish the distance between the scientific and popular language. It will become
easier for the unlearned to acquire English, and
for the learned to cultivate and improve the vernacular dialects. The languages of India will be
assimilated to the languages of Europe, as far as
the arts and sciences and general literature are
concerned; and mutual intercourse and the introduction of further improvements will thus be
facilitated. And, above all, the vernacular dia-

lects of India will, by the same process, be united
among themselves. This diversity of language is
one of the greatest existing obstacles to improvement in India. But when English shall every
where be established as the language of education,
when the vernacular literature shall every where
be formed from materials drawn from this source,
and according to models furnished by this proto-
type, a strong tendency to assimilation will be created. Both the matter and the manner will be
the same. Saturated from the same source, recast
in the same mould, with a common science, a common standard of taste, a common nomenclature,
the national languages, as well as the national character, will be consolidated ; the scientific and literary acquisitions of each portion of the community
will be at once thrown into a common stock for the
general good ; and we shall leave an united and enlightened nation, where we found a people broken up
into sections, distracted by the system of caste, even
in the bosom of each separate society, and depressed
by literary systems, devised much more with a view
to check the progress, than to promote the advance,
of the human mind. No particular effort is required
to bring about these results. They will take place
in the natural course of things by the extension of
English education, just as the inhabitants of the

greater part of Europe were melted down into one people by the prevalence of the Roman language and arts. All that is required is, that we should not laboriously interpose an obstacle to the progress of this desirable change by the forced cultivation of the Sanskrit and Arabic languages.

The argument we have been considering is the last hold of the oriental party. Forced to admit that Sanskrit and Arabic are not worth teaching for the knowledge they contain, they would obtain a reprieve for them on the ground that their vocabularies are required to patch up the vernacular dialects for the reception of Western knowledge. Discarded as masters, they are to be retained as servants to another and a better system. Their spirit has fled, but their carcase must be preserved to supply the supposed deficiencies, and to impair the real energies, of the system which is growing up in their place.

But, specious as the argument is, I should not have dwelt on it so long, if it had not been closely connected with a most pernicious error. The time of the people of India has hitherto been wasted in learning languages as distinguished from knowledge — mere words as distinguished from things — to an extent almost inconceivable to Europeans. This has been in a great measure unavoidable.

The Mahommedan legal system was locked up in Arabic; the Hindu in Sanskrit; Persian was the language of official proceedings; English that of liberal education and of a great part of our judicial and revenue system — all of these being independent of the common colloquial languages. If, therefore, a person learned only one foreign or dead language, it was impossible for him to qualify himself to take an efficient part in public business. If he learned several, his best years were wasted in the unprofitable task of studying grammar and committing vocabularies to memory. Persons were considered learned in proportion to the number of languages they knew; and men, empty of true knowledge and genius, acquired great reputations, merely because they were full of words. As great a waste of human time and labour took place in India under this state of things, as is caused in China by their peculiar system of writing. In one country, life was exhausted in learning the signs of words, and in the other in learning words themselves.

At first we gave decided encouragement to this false direction of the national taste. Our own attention was turned the same way. Oriental philology had taken the place of almost every other pursuit among our Indian literary men. The surprising copiousness, the complicated mechanism of the Sanskrit and Arabic languages were spoken of as if languages were an end to be attained, instead of a means for attaining an end, and were deserving of being studied by all sorts of people without any reference to the amount or kind of knowledge which they contain. All the concurrent systems were liberally patronised by the government, and the praises and emoluments lavished on great Arabic and Sanskrit scholars, were shared by natives as well as Europeans.

By degrees, however, a more wholesome state of things began to prevail. The government ceased to give indiscriminate support to every literary system, without reference to its real merits. Persian is ceasing to be the language of business. The study of Arabic and Sanskrit will soon be rendered superfluous by the inestimable boon which is being prepared for the people, of a complete body of law in their own language. By these changes an incalculable saving of human labour will be effected. The best literary, scientific, and professional education will be obtained at the expense of learning a single foreign language : and the years which were before painfully spent in breaking the shell of knowledge, will be employed in devouring the kernel.

But if it be really true that the cultivation of
the ancient classical languages is necessary to
qualify the popular dialects for the reception
of European knowledge, the progress of this
salutary change must be arrested in the midst;
the intellect of the country must be rechained to
the heavy burden which has, for so many ages,
prevented it from standing upright; and a pursuit which absorbs the time of the literary class, to
the exclusion of those studies which can alone
enable them to regenerate their country, must be
indefinitely persevered in. It is true that neither
the law, nor the administration of it, nor the
established system of public instruction, any longer
require this enormous sacrifice. But the phi-
lological system lately propounded by the advocates of Oriental education does require it. Such
is the expense at which this theory is to be maintained. If crores, instead of lacs of rupees, had
been spent in founding Sanskrit colleges and printing Sanskrit books, it would have been as nothing
compared with this. The mental and moral energies of India are to be kept for ages in a state of
worse than Egyptian bondage, in order that the
vernacular dialects may be improved from congenial, instead of from uncongenial, sources. The
ordinary terms on which the God of wisdom has

accorded knowledge to his creatures are thought too easy; and new and hitherto unheard-of conditions * are to be imposed, of such a nature as must effectually prevent the monopoly of learning, hitherto maintained in the East, from being broken in upon by the rapid diffusion of English education.

Another argument used by the Oriental party is, that little real progress can be made until the learned classes in India are enlisted in the cause of diffusing sound knowledge, and that "one able Pundit or Maulavee, who should add English to Sanskrit or Arabic, who should be led to expose the absurdities and errors of his own systems, and advocate the adoption of European knowledge and principles, would work a greater revolution in the minds of his unlettered countrymen than would result from their proficiency in English alone."

* The natives themselves have no idea of this alleged dependence of the vernacular languages upon the Sanskrit.   Mr. Adam observes, at page 77 of his last report, "There is no connection between the Bengalee and Sanskrit schools of Bengal, or between the Hindee and Sanskrit schools of Behar : the teachers, scholars, and instruction of the common schools are totally different from those of the schools of learning, the teachers and scholars being drawn from different classes of society, and the instruction directed to different objects.   But this remark does not apply to the Persian and Arabic schools, which are intimately connected, and which almost inperceptibly pass into each other ; " and to the same effect at greater length at page 59.

The first objection to this plan of reform is, that it is impracticable. An able Pundit or Maulavee can be formed only by a long course of instruction, extending far into the years of manhood. It is then too late to begin a new training in European literature and science, and even if it were not too late, they would have no inclination for the task. Their interest, their affections, their prejudices, their pride, their religious feelings are all pre-engaged in behalf of the systems under the influence of which they have grown up, and by which their minds have been formed. Their time of change is in every respect gone by. Although the system of education advocated by the oriental party had a fair trial of upwards of ten years, no teacher of this description was produced, nor was there ever any appearance of one. A few Maulavees and Pundits may, to please us, have acquired a superficial knowledge of a few of the most obvious parts of the European systems of geography and astronomy, but none of them showed any disposition to preach a crusade against the systems under which they had been brought up, and to which they were still as much attached as any of their class.

The next objection to this scheme is, that even if it were practicable, it is quite unnecessary. The

object for which it is proposed to raise up teachers
endowed with such rare qualifications, has been
already accomplished. A revolution has already
taken place in men's minds, not only among the
unlettered, but what is of far more consequence,
among the middle and upper classes, whose property, activity, and influence will secure the
further extension, and the permanence of the
change. The people are greedy for European
knowledge, and crowd to our seminaries in greater
numbers than we can teach them.   What more do
we want?   Where would have been the wisdom of entertaining the 1,200 English students
who besieged the doors of the Hooghly College
with lectures on the absurdities of the Pooranic
system of the earth? They already fully admitted the superiority of our system, and came
on purpose to be instructed in it; and so it is
with thousands of youth in every part of the
Bengal provinces.

It is in vain to direct our instructions to those
whose habits of mind are identified with the old
system, and whose reputation and subsistence depend on its continuance. If Luther had addressed
the Roman Catholic clergy, and Bacon the schoolmen, instead of the rising generation, and all who
were not strongly pre-engaged in behalf of any

system, we should have missed our European Reformation, both of philosophy and religion. Still less ought we to propagate the very systems, which it is our object to supplant, merely in the hope of being able to ingraft some shoots of European science upon them. Bacon did not educate schoolmen, nor Luther Roman Catholic priests, to become the instruments of their reforms. At this rate we should have been ever learning, and never able to come to a knowledge of the truth. The barren trunk and branches would have been always growing, while the exotic additions to this uncongenial stock, having no root in themselves, would have produced no fruit, however often they might have been renewed. Neither is it necessary or desirable to carry on war against the old system by direct attacks upon it, or by making offensive assertions of the superiority of our own. The ordinary effect of controversy is to excite hostility and bitterness of spirit. Ram Mohun Roy, who comes nearer to the idea of the reformed teacher of the orientalists than any body else who has appeared, was looked upon as an apostate by his party, and they were roused by his attacks to organise a regular opposition to his views.

What we have to do is, not to dispute, but to teach — not to prepossess the minds of the

natives with false systems, and to keep our good
instruction till it is too late to be of use, but to
get the start of their prejudices by educating
them, from the beginning, according to our own
views. We ought to cherish European learning,
which has already taken deep root and begun to
throw out vigorous shoots, leaving the trunk of
the old system to a natural and undisturbed de-
cay. The rising generation will become the
whole nation in the course of a few years. They
are all craving for instruction, and we may mould
their unoccupied and supple minds in any way
we please.

The ancient system of learning is so constituted
that while we have no assistance to expect, we
have, at the same time, no opposition to fear, from
its native professors. According to the theory of
Hinduism, Law, Philosophy and Divinity, are
the peculiar inheritance of the Brahmins, while
the study of other branches of literature and
science is open to the inferior castes. " But
practically," Mr. Adam observes, " Brahmins
monopolise not only a part, but the whole, of
Sanskrit learning. In the two Behar districts,
both teachers and students, without a single exception belong to that caste, and the exceptions
in the Bengal districts are comparatively few."

The Hindu system of learning is, in short, a close monopoly, which has been established by the Brahmins to secure their own pre-eminence. They make no proselytes, because they wish to have no rivals. Why therefore should we strive to extend this system beyond the limits which the Brahmins themselves wish? They have no notion of making it popular: their object is to confine it within the limits of the sacerdotal class. We, on the contrary, for a long time acted as if we desired to inundate the whole country with it. All the Brahmins aim at is, not to be interfered with in the exclusive enjoyment of their peculiar learning. The education of the mass of the people does not enter into their views: this great field is totally unoccupied; and we may establish on it our own machinery of public instruction, without clashing with any other interest.

Our plan is based on exactly opposite principles from that of the Brahmins. Our object is to promote the extension*, not the monopoly of

* The diffusive spirit of European learning is strikingly exemplified in the young men who are educated at our institutions. To convince others of the superiority of European knowledge, and to communicate that knowledge to them, is evidently regarded both as a duty and pleasure by them. It is a matter of course with them: their letters are full of it. Those who are rich establish, or aid in the establishment of schools: those who are

learning; to rouse the mind and elevate the character of the whole people, not to keep them in a state of slavish submission to a particular sect. The laity, the great body of the middle and upper classes of native society, are now, for the first time, invited to enjoy the benefits of a liberal education. The key of knowledge has been restored to them; and they have been compensated for their long exclusion, by having opened to them fields of science with which the

---

poor often devote their leisure hours to giving gratuitous instruction;—they all aid in the good work to the extent of their ability. There may be something of the zeal of new converts in this, and of a desire to secure their own footing by increasing the number of the followers of the new learning: but, whatever may be the motive, the practice shows that Sanskrit and English literature inspire exactly opposite views of relative duty; and that while one is eminently selfish and exclusive, the other is benevolent and diffusive in its tendency. I believe that, in the great majority of instances, the educated natives are actuated in promoting the spread of European learning by a sincere desire to benefit their countrymen, by communicating to them that from which they have themselves derived so much pleasure and advantage. The same class of persons are distinguished by their liberal support of the public charities at Calcutta,—a duty in which the native gentlemen who have been brought up under the old system miserably fail. We shall not be surprised at this, when we recollect that our literature is deeply impregnated with the spirit of our beneficent religion; and that even the modern philosophy, which rejects religion, or professes to supply motives of action independent of it, has for its avowed object the amelioration of the condition of the mass of mankind.

learning of the Brahmins is not to be compared. Wealth, numbers, influence, are on their side. The movement is becoming more and more irresistible; and the power of directing the public mind is passing from those who have exercised it for the last two thousand years to an entirely new set of men.

Although the knowledge of Sanskrit is confined to the Brahminical caste, the Brahmins are by no means practically limited to a studious and religious life: the majority of them, perhaps, get their subsistence by secular pursuits. The number of persons, therefore, devoted to the study of Sanskrit is surprisingly small when it is closely examined: the number of those who study Arabic is still smaller. The following table, extracted from Mr. Adam's report, shows the actual number of teachers and students of those languages, in five of the principal districts of Bengal and Behar: —

	ARABIC.		SANSKRIT.	
	Teachers.	Students.	Teachers.	Students.
Moorshedabad	2	7	24	153
Beerbhoom............	2	5	56	393
Burdwan	12	55	190	1358
South Behar	12	62	27	437
Tirhoot	6	29	56	214
Total ..	34	158	353	2555

These facts are in the highest degree encouraging. In the single town of Hooghly there are as many boys receiving a good English education as the largest number of Sanskrit and Arabic students in any one of the districts reported on by Mr. Adam. In the other four districts, the Oriental students do not exceed the average number of English scholars in those districts, in which our means of instruction have been tolerably organised. At Calcutta, where there are at least 6,000 boys learning English, the preponderance must be overwhelming on the side of European literature. If such be the relative position of Eastern and Western learning in India *, while the latter is yet in its infancy, how will it be when English education shall have approached its maturity?

Besides the 158 Arabic students, Mr. Adam found 3,496 youths learning Persian in the five districts examined by him. But, although Arabic and Persian literature is strictly Mahommedan,

* The number of persons who cultivate the learned Eastern languages, is certainly much smaller in the Western provinces than in Bengal or Behar. There may be a few more Arabic scholars in some of the principal towns; but Sanskrit is generally held in no esteem, and is very little attended to. Whole districts might be named in which it would be difficult to find an Arabic or Sanskrit student.

the majority of the scholars were Hindus;
" Is this comparative large number of Hindu
scholars" Mr. Adam continues " the effect of a
laudable desire to study a foreign literature placed
within their reach? Or is it the effect of an artificial stimulus? This may be judged by com-
paring the number of Hindu teachers and scholars
of Persian, which, until lately, was almost the exclusive language of local administration, with that
of Hindu teachers and scholars of Arabic, which is
not called into use in the ordinary routine of government. With regard to teachers; there is not a
single Hindu teacher of Arabic in the five districts: all are Mussulmans. With regard to scholars, there are only 9 Hindu to 149 Mussulman
students of Arabic, and consequently 2,087 Hindus
to 1,409 Mussulmans who are learning Persian.
The small comparative number of Arabic students
who are Hindus, and the large comparative number of the Persian scholars of the same class seem
to admit of only one explanation; viz., *that the
study of Persian has been unnaturally forced by the
practice of government; and it seems probable, that
even a considerable number of the Mussulmans who
learn Persian may be under the same artificial influence."* This is another proof, that the tendency of

our system has hitherto been to encourage not English but Mahommedan learning.

Persian has now ceased to be the official language; and, as it is not recommended by any other consideration, the study of it must soon die out. The inducement to learn Arabic will be greatly diminished, if it will not be altogether annihilated by the promulgation of a code.   Sanskrit will, for the same reason, be cultivated by a smaller number of persons than formerly; and the study of it will be confined to those Brahmins who wish to qualify themselves to be priests and astrologers. Meanwhile the tide has set in strongly in favour of English; and the popular inclination is seconded by a system of public instruction, which is daily becoming more extended and better organised : an advantage which the old learning never had.   The Brahminical monopoly of knowledge is now re-acting on those for whose benefit it was established; and the national curiosity, which had for so many ages been deprived of its natural gratification, is greedily availing itself of the new opening presented to it.   If this disposition of the people be only moderately gratified by the establishment so proper means of instruction, we may reasonably expect that ten years hence the number of person studying English will be in the proportion of ten

to one to those who will be studying the learned
Oriental languages.

Lastly; it is urged, that as we have succeeded
the native chiefs who were the natural patrons of
Indian learning, we are bound to give that aid to
Oriental scholars which they would have done
had they never been displaced by us.

To promote the spread of knowledge among
our subjects is undoubtedly one of the most sacred
duties which has devolved on us as the rulers of
India: but I cannot admit the correctness of the
test by which the Oriental party would determine
the kind of knowledge to be taught. Is it meant
that we are bound to perpetuate the system
patronised by our predecessors, merely because
it was patronised by them, however little it
may be calculated to promote the welfare of the
people? If it be so, the English rule would be
the greatest curse to India it is possible to conceive. Left to themselves, the inherent rottenness
of the native systems must, sooner or later, have
brought them to a close. But, according to this
view of the subject, the resources of European skill
are to employed in imparting to them a new principle of duration: knowledge is to be used to perpetuate ignorance — civilisation to perpetuate barbarism ; and the iron strength of the English Govern-

ment to bind faster still the fetters which have so
long confined the native mind. This is a new view
of our obligations; and, if it be a just one, it is to be
hoped that in pity to our subjects we shall neglect
this branch of our duties. Fortunately for them,
we have not thought it incumbent on us to act on
this rule in other departments of administration.
We have not adopted into our system barbarous
penal enactments and oppressive modes of collect-
ing the revenue because they happened to be
favourites with our predecessors. The test of what
ought to be taught is, truth and utility. Our predecessors consulted the welfare of their subjects to
the best of their information: we are bound to
do the same by ours. We cannot divest ourselves of this responsibility: the light of European
knowledge, and the diffusive spirit of European
benevolence give us advantages which our predecessors did not possess. A new class of Indian
scholars is rising under our rule, more numerous
and better instructed than those who went before
them; and, above all, plans are in progress for
enlightening the great body of the people as far as
their leisure will permit — an undertaking which
never entered into the imagination of any of the
former rulers of India.

CHAP. V.

Proofs that the Time has arrived for taking up the Question of National Education.—The Disuse of the Persian Language.—The many important Bearings of this Change.—The Codification of the Mahommedan and Hindu Law.—The increased Employment of the Natives—The concurrence of all Classes of the Community towards the Object.

MANY circumstances indicate that the time has arrived for taking up the question of Indian national instruction in a way in which it has never yet been taken up. Obstacles, which formerly prevented the Government from taking decisive steps, have disappeared : unexpected facilities have come to light. The mind of India has taken· a new spring. Substitutes are required to fill up the void created by the passing away of antiquated systems. The people want instruction : the Government wants well educated servants to fill the responsible situations which have been opened to the natives. Every thing concurs to prove that this important subject ought no longer to be regarded only as an amusement for the leisure hours of benevolent persons. It must now be taken up as a great public question, with that seriousness and resolution to make the necessary sacrifices which the interests at stake require.

Till lately the use of the Persian language in all official proceedings bound down the educated classes of the natives, in the Bengal and Agra presidencies, to the study of a thoroughly debasing and worthless literature, and the effect was the exclusion and degradation both of English and of the vernacular languages. This spell has been dissolved: the vernacular language has been substituted for the Persian throughout the revenue department; and the same measure is now in progress in the judicial department. The extraordinary ease and rapidity with which this change was effected in the revenue administration, proves that this event took place in the fullness of time, and furnishes a happy prognostic of future improvement. In Bengal, the Persian language had disappeared from the collectors' offices at the end of a month almost as completely as if it had never been used. It melted away like snow.

This measure has so many important bearings on the welfare of the people, and the character of our government, that I shall be excused for making a few remarks on it, although they will be

only indirectly connected with my subject. A
very general opinion has prevailed for some years
past, that Persian ought to be discarded; but
there was not the same concurrence of sentiment
as to what language ought to be substituted for it.
One party advocated the use of English, on the
ground, that it was of more importance that the
judges who had to decide a case should thoroughly
understand it, than the persons themselves who
were interested in it : that if the European officers
used their own language in official proceedings,
they would be much more independent of
the pernicious influence of their administrative
officers; and that the general encouragement
which would be given to the study of English, by
its adoption as the official language, would give a
powerful impulse to the progress of native enlightenment. Some years ago this opinion was the
prevailing one among those who were favourable
to the plan of giving the natives a liberal European
education; and it was even adopted by the Bengal
government, as will be seen by the extract at the
foot of the page*, from a letter from the secretary
in the Persian department, to the Committee of
Public Instruction, dated the 26th June, 1829.

* "One of the most important questions connected with the
present discussion is, that of the nature and degree of encourage-

Another party advocated the use of the vernacular language; and argued, that the substitution

---

ment to the study of the English language, which it is necessary and desirable for the Government to hold out independently of
providing books, teachers, and the ordinary means of tuition.
Your Committee has observed, that unless English be made the
language of business, political negotiation, and jurisprudence, it
will not be universally or extensively studied by our native subjects.—Mr. Mackenzie, in the note annexed to your Report, dated
the 3rd instant, urges strongly the expediency of a declaration by
Government, that the English will be eventually used as the language of business; otherwise, with the majority of our scholars, he
thinks, that all we 'do to encourage the acquisition must be
nugatory;' and recommends, that it be immediately notified, that,
after the expiration of three years, a decided preference will be
given to candidates for office, who may add a knowledge of
English to other qualifications. The Delhi Committee have also
advocated, with great force and earnestness, the expediency of
rendering the English the language of our Public Tribunals and
Correspondence, and the necessity of making known that such is
our eventual purpose, if we wish the study to be successfully and
extensively prosecuted.

" Impressed with a deep conviction of the importance of the subject,—and cordially disposed to promote the great object of
improving India, by spreading abroad the lights of European
knowledge, morals, and civilisation,—his Lordship in Council,
has no hesitation in stating to your Committee, and in authorising
you to announce to all concerned in the superintendence of your
native seminaries, that it is the wish and admitted policy of the
British Government to render its own language gradually and
eventually the language of public business throughout the country;
and that it will omit no opportunity of giving every reasonable
and practicable degree of encouragement to the execution of this
project. At the same time, his Lordship in Council, is not pre-
dared to come forward with any distinct and specific pledge as to

of one foreign language for another was not what was wanted ; that as fewer natives would know English than Persian for some time to come, the

---

the period and manner of effecting so great a change in the system of our internal economy ; nor is such a pledge considered to be at all indispensable to the gradual and cautious fulfilment of our views. It is conceived that, assuming the existence of that disposition to acquire a knowledge of English, which is declared in the correspondence now before Government, and forms the ground-work of our present proceedings, a general assurance to the above effect, combined with the arrangements in train for providing the means of instruction, will ensure our obtaining at no distant period a certain, though limited, number of respectable native English scholars ; and more effectual and decisive measures may be adopted hereafter, when a body of competent teachers shall have been provided in the Upper Provinces, and the superiority of an English education is more generally recognised and appreciated.

" As intimated, however, by the Delhi Committee, the use of the English in our public correspondence with natives of distinction, more especially in that which is of a complimentary nature, would in itself be an important demonstration in favour of the new course of study, as serving to indicate pretty clearly the future intentions of Government ; and there appears to be no objection to the immediate application of this incentive to a certain extent, and under the requisite limitations. The expediency, indeed, of revising the Governor General's correspondence with the higher classes of natives on the above principles, has before, more than once, under-gone discussion and consideration ; and the Governor-general in Council, deems the present a suitable occasion for resolving to address the native chiefs and nobility of India in the English lan-guage, (especially those residing in our own provinces,) whenever there is reason to believe, either that they have themselves acquired a knowledge of it, or have about them persons possessing that knowledge, and generally in all instances where the adoption of the new medium of correspondence would be acceptable and agreeable.

influence of the subordinate native officers would
be rather increased than diminished by the change;
that if the European officers were able to get
through their business without using the vernacular language, they would naturally neglect
the study of it; and that, although the plan proposed would give an artificial stimulus to the
study of English, it would condemn the vernacular
languages, the increased cultivation of which
was of still more importance, to continued exclusion and contempt. To these another argument has been added by the course of events;
which is, that as by the late changes in the judicial system every civil case may be decided in the
first instance by a native judge, the general introduction of English as the official language would
be nearly impracticable.

Every body is now agreed in giving the preference to the vernacular language. It is a great
point gained for the efficiency and popularity, and
consequently for the permanence of our rule, that
the European officers have now been placed in
such a position that they must make themselves
thoroughly acquainted with the language which
the people themselves speak.* All other media have

* The degree to which the European officers in Bengal are
ignorant of the popular language would hardly be credited.

been discarded, and public officers cannot discharge any of their duties unless they are familiar with it. As candidates for civil employ in India will now have only the vernacular language to attend to, the preparatory course of instruction ought to be lengthened and the examinations increased in strictness; and as, after they enter upon active life, almost every thing they hear, and speak, and read in the performance of their public duties, will be in the popular language, they must soon acquire the same, or nearly the same, facility of transacting business in it as in English.

This great point having been gained, every thing else will come out right. Being now brought into direct communication with the people, the European officers will be more independent of their executive officers: they will see and know

---

When I left Calcutta only one judge of the Sudder was believed to know it; and perhaps now there is not one. Every kind of judicial business was transacted in Persian, which is a language very unlike Bengalee; and the evidence of parties in criminal proceedings, which, by positive orders from the Court of Directors, is taken down in the language in which it is delivered, was, and perhaps still is, translated from the vernacular language into Persian, on the papers being submitted to the superior court. Public officers in the Upper Provinces were always acquainted with the vernacular language; and now that they have to transact business in it, they will become more familiar with it than ever.

more of the people, will take a greater interest
in their affairs, and will make their influence
more felt among them. The people, on the other
hand, will obtain a much better insight into what
is going on in the courts than it was possible for
them to do while the proceedings were conducted
in a foreign language. They will exercise a
greater check over the subordinate native officers.
They will be less in the hands of their own agents.
Justice will be better administered ; and the people
will have much more confidence in the administration of it. The field of selection for public employment, instead of being confined, as heretofore,
to those who were familiarly acquainted with the
Persian language, will be extended to every
educated person : entirely new classes of people
will be brought in to aid in the cheap and upright
administration of public affairs : individuals who,
without any higher literary attainment than a
good knowledge of their own language, have acquired in private life a character for ability and
integrity, and still more the young men who
have received at the public seminaries the best
education the country can afford, will infuse new
life and new morality into the system. As learn-
has ceased to be monopolised by the Brahmins,
so public employment has ceased to be mono-

polised by the class of people who are acquainted with Persian.

Lastly; by this measure a great impulse will be given to the study, not of English only, or of the vernacular language only, but both of English and of the vernacular language. Those natives who can afford to give their children a liberal education, will not cease to do so because it is no longer necessary to be acquainted with Persian. They are fully aware that the best educated persons generally succeed best in every pursuit of life; and in particular that they are appointed, in preference to others, to situations under Government. The vernacular language does not furnish the means of obtaining a liberal education : English does so in a much higher degree than any other language to which the natives of India have access; so much so, that the knowledge necessary for the practice of some professions — those of a Physician, a Surgeon, an Engineer, an Architect, and a Surveyor, for instance, — can be acquired through no other medium. These motives will be more than sufficient to stimulate the middle and upper classes of natives to the cultivation of English. Their own languages, on the other hand, have been relieved from the state of proscription and contempt to which they had been for ages condemned. They have been erected into the medium for transacting nearly the whole of the public business of the country. It will be an object to all — both to those who look forward to be employed in any situation under Government, and to those whose concerns bring them into connection with any public court or office — to have a competent knowledge of these languages. Those who receive any education will learn to read them. To write them with precision and elegance will be an attainment coveted by the most highly educated persons.

The changes which are taking place in the legal system of the country is another cause of the movement in native society. Buried under the obscurity of Sanskrit and Arabic erudition, mixed up with the dogmas of religion, and belonging to two concurrent systems made up of the dicta of sages of different ages and schools, the laws are at present in the highest degree uncertain, redundant, and contradictory. To obtain a moderate acquaintance with either Mahommedan or Hindu law is the work of a whole life, and is therefore the business of a separate profession, with which the bar and bench have nothing in common. The expositors of the law are the muftis and pundits; men, who deeply imbued with the spirit of the ancient

learning to which they are devoted, live only in
past ages, and are engaged in a perpetual struggle
to maintain the connection between the barbarism
of antiquity and the manners and opinions of the
present time. Their oracular responses are too
often the result of ignorance, pedantry, or corrup-
tion; but as they are few in number, and have a
monopoly of this kind of learning, it is almost impossible to convict them. The judges and bar-
risters, being excluded by the anomalous state of
the legal system from the mysteries of their own
profession, can exercise no control over them.
The people, who know no law except what happens
from time to time to fall from the lips of the muftis and pundits, are still more helpless. The inju-
rious influence of such a state of things as this, both
on the administration of justice and on the general
advancement of the people in knowledge and civilisation, can be better conceived than described.

This fabric has been overthrown by the decision of the British Parliament, that a Commission
should be appointed to ascertain and digest the laws
of India. The alliance between bad law and false
religion has been dissolved; and as the natives will
now be able to consider the civil and criminal codes
only as they affect their temporal welfare, the way
will be opened for the introduction of those fun-

damental changes in the frame-work of native society which are essential to its complete regeneration. The class of muftis and pundits, being no longer required, will cease to exist; and those who are learned in the law, and those who actually administer it, will for the future be the same persons. Legal knowledge will pass from pedants and antiquarians to persons who are engaged in the business and sympathise with the feelings of the present age. An improved bench and bar will both ensure a certain and prompt administration of the law, and give that aid to general improvement which may always be expected from a highly cultivated body of men, whose profession obliges them to be familiar with the interests, and attentive to the favour of society.

This happy change, however, will be slowly and imperfectly effected if it be not supported by corresponding arrangements in the department of public instruction. The Indian lawyers of the old school, who fortunately are not numerous, will be laid on the shelf on the promulgation of the new code. An entirely new set must be trained to take their place. It will be as easy now to give instruction in law as in any other branch of knowledge. Instead of an endless variety of contradictory maxims, there will be one plain consistent body of law.

Instead of legal knowledge being scattered through several languages—two of which are among the most difficult in the world—it will all be collected in our own language and in that of our native subjects.* The colleges established for giving instruction in Mahommedan and Hindu law, may now, in perfect accordance with their original design, be employed in educating enlightened men ; and the plan of education at all the other seminaries may be so arranged, that to whatever extent we succeed in improving the moral worth and cultivating the intellect of our subjects, to that same extent we shall provide materials for the pure and intelligent administration of the law.

Another great change has of late years been

* The difficulties in the way of giving legal instruction at the Government seminaries, which are now on the point of being removed, were thus noticed by the Education Committee, in their report for 1835 :—" Law would occupy the third place ; but at present this branch of instruction is attended with many difficulties, arising from the number of conflicting systems of law which prevail in this country, and the various languages in which they are embodied. The labours of the Law Commissioners, will, we hope, soon supply a condensed body of Anglo-Indian law, in the English and vernacular languages ; and it will then be proper to adopt measures to procure qualified legal instructors for each of our more important seminaries. We conceive that great advantages must result to the judicial administration from encouraging the best educated, who are also, we hope, the most moral and upright of the native youth, to seek employment in it."

made in our Indian administration, which ought
alone to excite us to corresponding exertions for
the education of the natives.   The system established by Lord Cornwallis was based upon the
principle of doing every thing by European agency.
Europeans are, no doubt, superior to the natives
in some of the most important qualities of adminis-
trators ; but the public revenue did not admit of
the employment of a sufficient number of them.
The wheels of Government therefore soon became
clogged : more than half of the business of the
country remained unperformed ; and at last it became necessary to abandon a plan, which, after a
fair trial, had completely broken down. The plan
which Lord William Bentinck substituted for it was,
to transact the public business by native agency,
under European superintendence ; and this change
is now in progress in all the different branches of
the administration. We have already native judges,
collectors, and opium and salt agents ; and it is now
proposed to have native magistrates.   The native
collectors are often vested with the same powers as
the European collectors ; and it has been lately
enacted, that all civil suits, of whatever amount,
may be tried in the first instance by the native
judges.

The success of this great measure depends en-

tirely on the fitness of the natives for the exercise
of the new functions to which they have been
called.   It is easier to dub a person collector or
magistrate, than to secure in him the possession
of the qualities which those offices require; and the
lowest imbecility as well as the highest efficiency
may be found under the same official title.   Measures have been adopted for educating native physicians ; and is it of less importance that native
judges should be professionally trained?   Care is
taken that the young Englishmen destined to hold
office in India are properly instructed ; and is no
exertion necessary to secure integrity and mental
cultivation in the native service, which now forms
at least as important a part of the general administration as the European officers themselves?
When the comparative state of morals and education in the classes from which the European and
native servants are respectively taken, is considered, it will appear that we could much better do
without the interference of the state with the previous training of the former than of the latter.   The
native functionaries have acquitted themselves extremely well, considering the corrupt school to
which most of them belonged and the suddenness
with which they were called to the performance
of new and important duties; but enough instances

of delinquency have occurred to prove, that the
country will not reap the full benefit of the change
that has been made, until we not only open prefer-
ment to the natives, but also furnish them with
the means by which they may merit that prefer-
ment, and learn how to use it; until we not only
give them power, but also secure, by a previous
training, the existence of those qualities with the
aid of which alone power can be beneficially exercised.

The necessity of the case obliged us to begin at
the wrong end, and we cannot too soon supply the
deficiency.   The business of the country is now
done; but we must strive that it should be well
done. There is now a sufficient number of judges
and collectors; but we must endeavour to provide
a succession of honest and well instructed judges
and collectors. We want native functionaries of a
new stamp, trained in a new school; and adding
to the acuteness, patience, and intimate acquaintance with the language and manners of the people which may always be expected in natives,
some degree of the enlightened views and integrity of character which distinguish the European
officers.   Our national interest and honour, our
duty to our subjects, and even justice to our native servants themselves, require this at our hands

These, however, are no new sentiments : they have
been repeatedly urged by the Court of Directors
on the Indian government; and considering how
deeply the success of our administration, not in
one only, but in all its different branches, is concerned in the establishment of a system of public
instruction adequate to the existing wants of the
country, it may be hoped that the necessary funds
will soon be placed at the disposal of the Governor-
general in Council.

But this part of the subject has another, and
perhaps a still more important aspect. The same
means which will secure for the Government a body
of intelligent and upright native servants, will stimulate the mental activity, and improve the morals
of the people at large. The Government cannot
make public employment the reward of distinguished merit, without encouraging merit in all
who look forward to public employ : it cannot
open schools for educating its servants, without
diffusing knowledge among all classes of its
subjects. Those who take their notions from England, or even from most of the Continental nations,
can have no conception what an immensely powerful engine, either for good or evil, an Asiatic government is. In India, the Government is every-
thing. Nearly the whole rental of the country

passes into its coffers.   Its civil and military establishments are on the largest scale.   The mercan-
tile, medical, sacerdotal, and other professions,
which absorb the greater part of our English youth
of the middle class, are either held in low esteem,
or are confined, at present, to particular castes;
and almost the only idea which a liberally educated
native has of rising in life, is by attaching himself
to the public service.   The Government, therefore,
by the power which it possesses of stimulating and
directing the minds of those who look forward to
public employ, is able to stimulate and direct the
mind of the whole nation.   The candidates for
situations in the public service comprise the largest
and best portion of the educated class; and the
educated class always draws after it the rest of the
people.

A plan has lately been suggested* to the Su-

* The Sudder Dewanee Adawlut, in their report for 1836,
strongly represented the necessity of securing a regular supply of
properly educated young men for employment in the judicial department; and the Education Committee, to whom the subject was
referred, suggested the plan above described.   The remarks of the
Sudder Dewanee Adawlut, are as follows: —

" The reports of the local authorities generally, however, speak
favourably of these two grades of native judges.   Regarding the
moonsiffs, there appears to be a greater difference of opinion, but,
under experienced and efficient Judges, the Court entertain hopes
that the moonsiffs will be ultimately found to perform their duty
in a correct and satisfactory manner.

preme Government, by the Education Committee,
by which this immensely important influence may

" With a view, however, of introducing a better educated class of
individuals into this office, the Court have directed me to state, that
they are of opinion, that some well-considered system should be
immediately adopted by Government, for the purpose of securing
a regular succession of duly qualified native judicial officers. No
peculiar acquirements are at present looked for in a native Judge,
beyond general good character, respectability of family, and
a competent knowledge of the Persian and Bengalese languages. No liberal or polite education, no legal acquirements,
no knowledge even of the general forms and rules of practice,
prescribed by the regulations of Government, is generally possessed
by any candidate for office, save perhaps in the latter instance by
some few individuals, who have been attached to the courts in
subordinate situations, as mohurrers, or moonshees, or vakeels,
and who are, therefore, well acquainted with the general routine
of our proceedings.

" As the readiest mode of improving the present system of no-
mination, the Court would suggest the appointment of a regular
professor, at all the Government Colleges, for the purpose of instructing the native youth in the laws and regulations of government, and for enabling the young men brought up at these institutions to qualify themselves for the judicial and revenue branches
of the public service. To each college possessing such a professor, whether, indeed, supported by Government or otherwise,
and whether in Calcutta or at any city in the interior, one or two
moonsiffships and uncovenanted deputy collectorships might be
presented as prizes every year, and these prizes should be bestowed
on any native youth, above the age of twenty-five years, who
might be found duly qualified, on public examination, for the
situation; the name of the successful candidate should then be
placed on the records of this court, in order that he might be employed in Bengal or Behar, according to his parentage, directly a
vacancy occurred; and in the mean time he should be obliged to

be applied to the development of the mind and
morals of our subjects, in the most extensive, effectual, and unobjectionable manner.   It is proposed
that public examinations should be annually held
at each of the great towns in the Bengal and Agra
presidencies, by officers appointed to make the cir-
cuit of the country for that purpose; that these
examinations should be open to all comers, wherever they may have been educated; that those
who acquit themselves well should be ranked according to their merit; and that the list so arranged, together with the necessary particulars
regarding the branches of knowledge in which
each person distinguished himself, should be sent
to the neighbouring functionaries, to enable them
to fill up from it the situations in their gift which

---

continue his legal studies at the college, a monthly personal
allowance of sixteen or twenty rupees being granted to him by
Government for his support.   The Court would further recommend that the monthly salaries of the moonsiffs be fixed at
150 rupees.   The very important duties now confided to the
native Judges undoubtedly renders the adoption of some systematic plan of education for these officers indispensably necessary; and
the Court therefore beg to urge that these suggestions may receive
the early consideration of Government."

After this, the abolition of the use of Persian was resolved
on; and the only real obstacle to the accomplishment of the wishes
of the Judges of the Sudder Dewanee was thus removed.

fall vacant. The European officers generally take so little interest in the disposal of their patronage, and are often so much at a loss for qualified candidates, that they would gladly avail themselves of this mode of replenishing the lower grades of the native service. After the young men had once been appointed, their further progress would, of course, depend upon their merits and length of service.

This plan, it will be observed, rests on a much wider basis than the Government seminaries. It is intended to encourage and reward mental cultivation wherever it exists; and to engage in the service of the country the best talent the country can afford, without any reference to particular places of education. The impulse, therefore, will be communicated to all alike. The boy from a public school will be brought into competition with the boy who has been educated in his father's house. The students from the Government colleges will contend with the young men brought up in the missionary seminaries. The Hindus and Mahommedans will vie with Christians of every denomination. There will be no distinction made, except that of superior merit. The emulation among the young men will extend to the conductors of the seminaries at which they are trained: the merits and defects of dif

ferent plans of education will become apparent
from the result of the annual examinations, and
those which are found to be most successful will
be generally adopted.   The striking effects produced by literary competition, when much less free
than this, and excited by much inferior rewards,
will give some idea of what may be expected from
a competition which will be open to all classes of
our Indian subjects, and will be stimulated by all
the influence and patronage of the Indian government.

But the most decisive proof that the time has
arrived for taking up the subject of national education is, that all classes of the community are now
ready to co-operate with the Government. A few
years ago, the education of the natives was regarded
by the Europeans either with aversion or contempt,
as they happened to consider it as a dangerous interference with native prejudice, or as a chimerical
undertaking unworthy of a man of sense. Now
there are few stations at which there are not one or
more European officers, who would be glad of an
opportunity of aiding the Committee in the prosecution of its plans.   The discussions which
took place between the advocates of the rival systems, by strongly drawing attention to the question, and, in a manner, forcing people to an

examination of it, greatly contributed to this result. All are now more or less interested and well informed on the subject; and what is of still more importance, all are of one mind about it, and have a settled and well understood plan to pursue. Whatever differences of opinion may linger among retired Indians in England, there are none now in India; or, at least, the adherents of the old system form such an exceedingly small minority, that it is unnecessary to mention them when speaking of the general sense of the European community.

The Missionaries, taking advantage of the prevailing feeling, have established numerous excellent seminaries, at which many thousand native youth are receiving a sound, and in some cases a liberal English education. English, Scotch, Americans, and Germans, concur in availing themselves of the English language as a powerful instrument of native improvement. English priests, lately sent from Rome to take charge of the Roman Catholic Christians of Portuguese and native descent, have had recourse to the same means for enlightening their numerous and degraded flocks. The Portuguese language (another instance of the confusion of tongues which has so long distracted and dissipated the mind of India) has been discarded from the churches and schools:

an English Liturgy has been introduced, and large English seminaries have been established. There are also institutions at which the youth of English and of mixed English and native descent receive as good a scientific and literary education as is consistent with the early period at which they enter into active life. Most of our schoolmasters have been drawn from this class; and, as they possess the trustworthiness and a great degree of the energy of the European character, combined with an intimate acquaintance with the native habits and language, they are no mean auxiliaries in the cause of native education.*

This harmony of effort, however, would be of little avail if it were not founded on a real desire on the part of the natives themselves to obtain the benefit of European instruction. The curiosity of the people is thoroughly roused, and the passion for English knowledge has penetrated the most obscure, and extended to the most remote parts of India. The steam boats, passing up and down the Ganges, are boarded by native boys, begging, not

---

* The institutions which have rendered most service in this way are, the Verulam Academy, the Parental Academic Institution, the High School, and the Military Orphan Asylum. Similar assistance may now be expected from the noble foundation of General Martin, and a large Proprietory School which has lately been established in the Himalaya Mountains.

for money, but for books.* The chiefs of the Punjab, a country which has never been subdued by the British arms, made so many applications to the Political Agent on the frontier to procure an English education for their children, that the Government has found it necessary to attach a schoolmaster to his establishment. The tide of literature is even rolling back from India to Persia, and the Supreme Government lately sent a large supply of English books for the use of the King of Persia's military seminary, the students of which were reported to be actuated by a strong zeal for European learning. The extent to which the Pasha of Egypt is engaged in enlightening his subjects, through the medium of English and the other European languages, is too well known to

* Some gentlemen coming to Calcutta were astonished at the eagerness with which they were pressed for books by a troop of boys, who boarded the steamer from an obscure place, called Comercolly. A Plato was lying on the table, and one of the party asked a boy whether that would serve his purpose. " Oh yes," he exclaimed, " give me any book ; all I want is a book." The gentleman at last hit upon the expedient of cutting up an old *Quarterly Review*, and distributing the articles among them. In the evening, when some of the party went ashore, the boys of the town flocked round them, expressing their regret that there was no English school in the place, and saying that they hoped that the Governor-general, to whom they had made an application on the subject when he passed on his way up the country, would establish one.

need any detail. The time has certainly arrived
when the ancient debt of civilisation which Europe
owes to Asia* is about to be repaid; and the sciences, cradled in the East and brought to maturity
in the West, are now by a final effort about to
overspread the world.†

* The early civilisation of Greece by settlers from Phœnicia
and Egypt ; the philosophical systems of Pythagoras and Plato ;
the knowledge of chemistry, medicine, and mathematics, which
emanated in a later age from the Arabian schools of Cordova
and Salerno, attest the obligations we are under to the Eastern
world. The greatest boon of all, our admirable system of arith-
metical notation, which has facilitated in an incalculable degree
the improvement of the sciences and the transaction of every
kind of business for which the use of numbers is requisite,
is distinctly traceable through the Arabs to the Hindus : we call
it the Arabian, the Arabs call it the Hindu system, and the
Hindus attribute the invention of it to their gods. It has been
practised in India from a period which precedes all written and
traditionary memorials.

† It may be as well to mention some of the probable causes of
the existing state of native feeling on this subject. The first is the
same which gave rise to the revival of learning, and the cultivation
of the vernacular languages in Europe, or the increase in the number and importance of the middle class of society. External peace,
internal security of property, arising from a regular administration of justice, increased facilities to trade, the permanent settlement of the land revenue of the Lower, and a long settlement of
that of the Upper Provinces, have all contributed to raise up a class
between the nabob and the ryot, which derives its consequence from
the exercise   industry and enterprise, which is possessed of the leisure necessary for literary pursuits, and which, being a creation of
our won, is naturally inclined to imitate us, and to adopt our views.
Secondly, The people feeling themselves safe in their persons and

property, and being relieved from the harassing anxieties which daily attend those who live under a barbarous arbitrary government, enjoy that peace of mind, without which it is impossible that letters can be successfully cultivated. Thirdly, The natives cannot fail to be struck by our moral and intellectual superiority ; and they are led, by the combined influence of curiosity and emulation, to search for the causes of it in our literature. This motive has led the Russians and Turks, and other entirely independent nations, to cultivate foreign literature; and it cannot, therefore, excite wonder that the Hindus, who stand in such a close relation to us, should have been influenced by it. Fourthly, A liberal English education is the surest road to promotion. It is by far the best education the natives can get ; and the Government must always select the best instructed persons that are to be had, for the public service. Lastly, The Hindus have always been a literary people ; but as the body of the nation were shut out by the Brahmins from all participation in their own learning, they eagerly avail themselves of what is now offered by us to their acceptance, recommended as it is by so many attractions.

I

CHAP. VI.

*The Establishment of a Seminary at each Zillah Sta-
tion, a necessary Preliminary to further Operations.
— The Preparation of Books in the Vernacular Languages. — A Law of Copyright required. — Native
Education in the Madras and Bombay Presidencies.
— The Establishment of a comprehensive System of
public Instruction for the whole of British India
urgently required. — The public Importance of a
separate Provision being made for the Prosecution of
Researches into ancient Asiatic Literature.*

To proceed to practical details ; all we have to do
is, to follow out the plan which has been steadily
pursued since March, 1835. Seminaries have been
established at the head stations of about half the
Zillahs in the Bengal and Agra presidencies ; and
the first thing to be done is, to establish similar institutions in the remaining forty Zillahs. At the average rate of 250 rupees per mensem for each seminary, this would require an annual addition to the
fund of 120,000 rupees, or about £12,000 a-year.*

* As the supply of educated persons increases, schoolmasters
will be obtained at lower salaries; and the saving arising from this
source, and from the falling in of stipends to students, may be
applied to the improvement of the seminaries. This is inde-

Whatever system of popular instruction it may
hereafter be resolved to organise in India, these
Zillah seminaries must form the basis of it; and,
as some time must be allowed for their operation before we can with advantage proceed a
step further, their early establishment is a matter of importance. Every part of our dominions having the same claim upon us, there is
exactly the same reason for establishing a central school in one Zillah as in another. Indeed, the motives for carrying out the plan
to its full extent are much stronger than those
for originally commencing it. The inhabitants
of a Zillah in which a seminary has been for
some time established, have a very unfair advantage given them over the inhabitants of the
neighbouring Zillahs. Calcutta has lately been
supplying native deputy-collectors to the whole of
Bengal and Behar, because it was the only place
at which educated natives were to be obtained in
any number. This was justified by the emer-
gency of the case; but, as a general rule, it is
very desirable to employ the natives as much as
possible in their own neighbourhood. Strangers,

pendent of the contributions of the European and native community, and of the boys themselves, which will never be found defi-
cient where the Government sets an example of liberality.

invested with power, are looked upon with jealousy; and they are generally in a hurry to make what they can, and return to their own homes.   On the other hand, respectable natives are more easily induced to take service, and are more under the control of public opinion in their own district than elsewhere.

The next step will be, to extend the system from town to country; from the influential few to the mass of the people.   This part of the subject is not of pressing importance, because the materials of a national system must be prepared in the Zillah seminaries before they can be employed in the organisation of the Purgunnah and village schools.   The youth of the upper and middle classes, both in town and country, will receive such an education at the head station of the Zillah as will make them willing and intelligent auxiliaries to us hereafter in extending the same advantages to the rest of their countrymen.   The Zillah seminaries will be the normal schools, in which a new set of village schoolmasters will be trained, and to which many of the existing schoolmasters will be induced to resort to obtain new lights in their profession.   The books and plans of instruction, which have been tried and found to answer at the Zillah seminaries, will be introduced into the Purgunnah and village schools. In short, the means of every description for establishing a system of national instruction, will be accumulated at these central points; and our future operations are likely to be unembarrassed and efficacious in proportion as this foundation is well and securely laid. We have, at present, only to do with outlines, but they should be drawn with a strict reference to the details which will hereafter have to be filled in.

A great deal has been said about the importance of preparing books in the vernacular languages; and it has been even urged as a proof that there is something unsound in our plan of operations, that there is a greater demand for English books than for books in the vernacular languages.* This objection seems to me to arise from a disposition to anticipate the natural course of events. There

* It appears from the following contrasted statement, taken from the two last biennial reports of the School-book Society, that the demand for books in the vernacular languages is increasing, although not as yet in so great a degree as that for English books: —

	1832 and 1833.	1834 and 1835.
Hindusthanee	1,077	3,384
Hinduee	1,514	4,171
Bengalee	4,896	5,754
Orissa	815	834
	7,302	14,143

is at present only a limited demand for books in the vernacular languages. But what is the remedy proposed?—To print more books. To print more books than are wanted, because they are not wanted! This scheme, though in appearance more popular, would be, in reality, just as useless as that of the Arabic translations: the books would rot on the shelves; and, as they would not be read, nothing would be gained by their being in a known, instead of an unknown, tongue. The chance that anything worth reading will be produced by salaried translators, who are certain of being paid whether their books are good or bad, is also very small indeed. If such a plan were to answer in any degree, it would be likely to do so at the expense of pitching the national taste at the outset at a very low standard.

In order to create a vernacular literature, we must begin by creating a demand for one. The adoption of the vernacular language, as the language of public business, will contribute more towards the formation of a vernacular literature than if the Government were to spend a crore of rupees in translating and printing books. It will have the same effect as the substitution of English for Norman-French in legal proceedings, and for Latin in the exercises of religion had in England.

We must also give a liberal English education to
the middle and upper classes, in order that we
may furnish them with both the materials and the
models for the formation of a national literature.
In this way, the demand, and the means of supplying the demand, will grow up together. The class
of people who, without knowing English, require
some mental aliment, will become more and more
extensive : the class who do know English, will
be more and more induced by pecuniary interest,
by ambition, by the desire of doing good, to supply this aliment. Out of their fulness, from minds
saturated with English knowledge and tastes
formed by the study of English masterpieces,
they will produce, not dull translations, but original works, suited to the intellectual habits of their
countrymen. Mediocrity will meet with no encouragement. Out of many attempts, few will succeed;
but those few will lay the foundation of the mental independence of India, and will oblige even
those who know English to regard their own literature with respect, and to consider it as worthy
of cultivation for its own sake.

Latin was formerly upheld as the only proper
medium for scientific and literary composition.
Petrarch expected to be known to posterity by
his Latin poems, which nobody now reads : and of

all Bacon's works, his Essays, which he wrote in
English as an amusement for his leisure hours,
are alone in everybody's hands; but, notwithstanding this, the modern European literature
will be found to have taken its great start at
the time when the cultivation of the classical languages was at its height. To check the study
of Latin at that period would have been to
check the progress of knowledge, of taste, and of
curiosity, which, descending lower and lower, at
last gave rise to the admirable literature of the
West. To check the study of English, in order
to force that of the vernacular language, would
have an equally bad effect upon the nascent literature of India. It would retard the process of
national improvement by a fruitless endeavour
to have that first, which ought, in the natural
course of things, to come last: it would have
the same effect on the increase of knowledge
which the mistaken policy of some nations has on
the increase of wealth, who, impatient to have manufactures before they come in their own time,
divert a portion of their capital from the more profitable employment of agriculture to the less profitable one of manufactures.

There is, however, one mode in which the
Government may, without running any risk of en-

couraging mediocrity, give direct aid to the growth of a national literature. The consumption of books in the native languages, in the Government schools, is already great, and is daily increasing as the schools become more numerous and better filled. The adoption of any book as a class-book in the Government seminaries also establishes its reputation, and creates a general demand for it. Here then is a certain and perfectly unobjectionable mode of encouraging the production of good books : only the best books of each kind are bought, and they are bought only as they are actually wanted; the pupils themselves pay for them, and a large number of useful books thus annually pass into the hands of the people. When particular books are required for the use of the Government schools, it would be advisable to make the want publicly known, in order that all native authors may have an opportunity of supplying it. The best among many competitors is likely to produce something better worth having than any single writer who could be selected.

A good law of copyright, embracing the whole of British India, would now be of great use. The want has only lately begun to be felt. Nothing was to be made by works in manuscript; and printed books were not in sufficient demand to make the copyright of any value. Now, however, large editions of many works, both in English and the vernacular languages, are called for; and anxiety is felt by publishers on account of their liability to be deprived of their profits by piratical editions.

Although my remarks have been particularly directed to the state of things in the Bengal and Agra presidencies, they are, for the most part, equally applicable to the rest of British India. The plan which has been found to be best adapted for enlightening the people in Bengal, is not likely to be less efficacious at Madras and Bombay. Those presidencies will suffer less by the start of a few years, which Bengal has had, than they will gain by being placed in possession of a well devised and well tested plan of proceeding, without having had any of the trouble or expense of making the experiment.

At Madras, where least has been done for native education, there are, perhaps, more abundant materials and fewer obstacles than in any of the other presidencies. Native learning is even more thinly spread than in Bengal, and no institutions have been established by us to confirm its hold upon the country. On the other hand, a colloquial knowledge of English is a much more common acquirement than it is in Bengal. There are several different languages spoken in the Madras presidency, and English has been to a great extent adopted as the common medium of intercourse, not only between Europeans and natives, but between the natives themselves. This circumstance must give a permanent impulse to the study of the language, and will probably lead to its being more commonly used in ordinary conversation, and more largely diffused through the native languages in the south of India than in any other part of our Eastern dominions. The rough materials of a system of national education are therefore ready to hand in the Madras presidency; and all we have to do is to organise them, and apply them to their proper purpose. English is no novelty; it is in great request; thousands already know it: but it has hitherto been taught loosely and unsystematically, and we must bring all the modern improvements in education to the aid of its easy and correct acquisition. It has hitherto been taught merely to the extent necessary for carrying on colloquial intercourse; but we must enable our subjects to cultivate it as the means of obtaining access to all the knowledge of Europe.

At Bombay more has been done for native education. At first, too exclusive attention was paid to the vernacular languages; books for which there was no demand, were translated at a heavy expense; and as the vernacular language only was taught in the schools, a fixed and narrow limit was placed to the acquisitions of the pupils. This plan has since been modified; and, while proper attention is still paid to the vernacular language, English is also extensively cultivated: the taste for it is said to be rapidly increasing; and as the youth of the Bombay Presidency have every thing at their disposal which the English language contains, they have now an open career before them.

It is a striking confirmation of the soundness of the prevailing plan of education, that the Bengal and Bombay Presidencies, although they set out from opposite quarters, and preserved no concert with each other, settled at last on exactly the same point. In Bengal we began by giving almost exclusive attention to the native classical languages, as they did in Bombay to the vernacular languages; and in both cases experience has led to a conviction of the value of English, and to its having had that prominent place accorded to it which its importance demands. It is time that these partial efforts should give place to a general plan, embracing the whole of British India. The constitution given to it by the late charter has es-

tablished the identity of our Indian empire, and
the Government has since been occupied in remo-
delling the different departments of administration
on this principle. All the provinces of this empire
are to have the same criminal and civil law, the
same post-office and commercial regulations; and
it is surely not of less importance that they should
have the same system of public instruction. Our
subjects have set out on a new career of improvement: they are about to have a new character
imprinted on them. That this national movement
should be taken under the guidance of the State,
that the means at our disposal should be equally
distributed, that each province should profit by
the experience of all the rest, that there should
be one power to regulate, to control, to urge the
indolent, to restrain the over-zealous, to lead on
the people by the same or corresponding means
to the same point of improvement, will hardly
be denied to be as conducive to the welfare of
our subjects as it will be to the popularity and
permanency of our dominion over them.

The Bengal Education Committee was bound
to keep a single eye to the enlightenment of the
people, that being the object for which they had
been associated as a public body, and for which
the administration of a portion of the reve-

nue had been committed to their hands. The
general interests of science formed no part of
their public charge, but it must not be supposed
that they were on that account personally indifferent to them.   No men are more disposed than
the members of the Education Committee to ad-
mire the exertions of James Prinsep, of Hodgson,
of Turner, of Masson, or are more anxious to
contribute to their success in any way that does
not involve a sacrifice of public duty.   The gentlemen whom I have named, and others who are
associated with them, are turning the ancient
Arabic and Sanskrit records to their proper account. Owing to the vastly superior means now at
our disposal, they are worse than useless, considered
as a basis of popular education; but as a medium
for investigating the history of the country, and
the progress of mind and manners during so many
ages, they are highly deserving of being studied and
preserved.   These two objects have no more to do
with each other than the Royal Society has with
Mr. Wyse's Committee on National Education, or
the societies for Preserving Welch and Gaelic Literature, with the British and Foreign School Society.
By joining them in a forced and unnatural union
the progress of both has been retarded.   Philo-
logical and antiquarian research was supported on

the resources of education. Education was conducted in a way more adapted for the lecture-room
of a German university, than for the enlightenment of benighted Asiatics. The friends of education, in performing the indispensable duty of
recovering the sum which had been assigned by
the state for their object, were very unwillingly
placed in a state of apparent opposition to the
interests of oriental research. The more immediate supporters of the Asiatic Society, in strug-
gling to retain the interest they had enjoyed in
this sum, were marshalled against the cause of
popular education. Since the separation has been
effected, both parties have pursued their respective
objects with much greater success than before.
The Education Committee, uninfluenced by any
foreign bias, has employed all its disposable funds
in founding new seminaries. The Asiatic Society,
forced at last to lean on its natural supporters,
has been liberally assisted by private contributions;
and will, it may be hoped, soon receive that aid
from the public resources to which the public
importance of its labours so justly entitle it.

It is much to be desired that this division of
labour between the departments of general science
and popular education should receive the sanction
of the highest authority, and be carried into full

effect. The plan which appears to me best calculated to answer every purpose, is, for the Government to attach a Sanskrit professor, with several
native assistants, to the establishment of the Asiatic
Society. These persons, selected on account of
their eminent attainments and known love of science,
and undisturbed by any other pursuit, might devote themselves to the investigation of the history,
antiquities, philosophy, and literature of the East,
recording the result of their researches in the most
lasting and available forms. India is undoubtedly
at the threshold of a new era; and it seems to be
no less incumbent on us at this period to gather
up the recollections of the past, than to provide
matter of national improvement for the future.
The Hindu system of learning has formed the
character of the people up to the present point;
and it must still be studied, to account for daily
occurring phenomena of habits and manners.
Whatever mental cultivation, whatever taste
for scientific and literary pursuits has survived
among the Hindus, is owing to it: they were a
literary people when we were barbarians; and,
after centuries of revolution, and anarchy, and
subjection to foreign rule, they are still a literary
people, now that we have arrived at the highest
existing point of civilisation. That the system

which has produced these effects should be carefully analysed and recorded in all its different
parts, is no less required by the interests of science
in general than by our particular interest as rulers
of India. The pundits and students of the Sanskrit College, whose whole time is taken up in
teaching and learning that language, are quite
unequal to the task. The Asiatic Society, whose
proper business it is, are also at present unequal
to it; they have no machinery for its performance : the members of the society are principally
public officers, overburdened with other duties;
and they have as yet been obliged to confine their
attention to the replenishment of their museum,
and the collection of such scattered notices of the
antiquities of the country as have been sent to them
by amateur correspondents. The examining and
laying open of the different branches of Hindu and
Mahommedan literature, has been of necessity,
almost entirely neglected; and unless some plan
be adopted such as I have suggested, it is not
easy to see how this object (the one for which the
society was principally founded), can ever be accomplished. Such Arabic and Sanskrit works
as are worthy of being preserved, might be printed
under the superintendence of the professor and his
native assistants ; and the expense might be borne,

as hitherto, partly by subscription, and partly by the sale of the works themselves, without much assistance from Government. What the finances of the society are not equal to, is, the payment of salaries sufficient to secure the whole time of highly qualified persons to review and make researches into the ancient literature of the country.

Having made this provision for the preservation of Arabic and Sanskrit learning, and satisfied every reasonable wish which either national pride or scientific curiosity can suggest, we shall be able with more satisfaction to take the requisite steps for the introduction of new knowledge, and the creation of a new literature. Every object will have been secured, and all parties will pursue their respective ends without interfering, and will co-operate without misunderstanding.

CHAP. VII.

*The Political Tendency of the different Systems of
Education in use in India.*

THERE can be no dispute as to what our duty as
the rulers of India requires us to do. But it has
been said, and may be said again, that whatever
our duty may be, it is not our policy to enlighten
the natives of India; that the sooner they grow
to man's estate, the sooner they will be able to do
without us; and that by giving them knowledge,
we are giving them power, of which they will make
the first use against ourselves.

If our interest and our duty were really opposed
to each other, every good man, every honest Englishman, would know which to prefer. Our national experience has given us too deep a sense of
the true ends of government, to allow us to think
of carrying on the administration of India except
for the benefit of the people of India. A nation
which made so great a sacrifice to redeem a few
hundred thousand negroes from slavery, would
shudder at the idea of keeping a hundred millions
of Indians in the bondage of ignorance, with all

its frightful consequences, by means of a political
system supported by the revenue taken from the
Indians themselves.   Whether we govern India
ten or a thousand years, we will do our duty by
it : we will look, not to the probable duration of
our trust, but to the satisfactory discharge of it,
so long as it shall please God to continue it to us.
Happily, however, we are not on this occasion
called upon to make any effort of disinterested
magnanimity.   Interest and duty are never really
separated in the affairs of nations, any more than
they are in those of individuals; and in this case
they are indissolubly united, as a very slight examination will suffice to show.

The Arabian or Mahommedan system is based
on the exercise of power and the indulgence of
passion.   Pride, ambition, the love of rule, and of
sensual enjoyment, are called in to the aid of religion.   The earth is the inheritance of the Faithful : all besides are infidel usurpers, with whom
no measures are to be kept, except what policy
may require.   Universal dominion belongs to the
Mahommedans by Divine right.   Their religion
obliges them to establish their predominance by the
sword; and those who refuse to conform are to be
kept in a state of slavish subjection.   The Hindu
system, although less fierce and aggressive than

the Mahommedan, is still more exclusive: all who are not Hindus are impure outcasts, fit only for the most degraded employments; and, of course, utterly disqualified for the duties of government, which are reserved for the military, under the guidance of the priestly caste. Such is the political tendency of the Arabic and Sanskrit systems of learning. Happily for us, these principles exist in their full force only in books written in difficult languages, and in the minds of a few learned men; and they are very faintly reflected in the feelings and opinions of the body of the people. But what will be thought of that plan of national education which would revive them and make them popular; would be perpetually reminding the Mahommedans that we are infidel usurpers of some of the fairest realms of the Faithful, and the Hindus, that we are unclean beasts, with whom it is a sin and a shame to have any friendly intercourse. Our bitterest enemies could not desire more than that we should propagate systems of learning which excite the strongest feelings of human nature against ourselves.

The spirit of English literature, on the other hand, cannot but be favorable to the English connection. Familiarly acquainted with us by means of our literature, the Indian youth almost cease to

regard us as foreigners. They speak of our great
men with the same enthusiasm as we do. Educated in the same way, interested in the same objects, engaged in the same pursuits with ourselves,
they become more English than Hindus, just as
the Roman provincials became more Romans than
Gauls or Italians. What is it that makes us what
we are, except living and conversing with English
people, and imbibing English thoughts and habits
of mind? They do so too: they daily converse
with the best and wisest Englishmen through the
medium of their works; and form, perhaps, a
higher idea of our nation than if their intercourse
with it were of a more personal kind. Admitted
behind the scenes, they become acquainted with
the principles which guide our proceedings; they
see how sincerely we study the benefit of India in
the measures of our administration; and from violent opponents, or sullen conformists, they are
converted into zealous and intelligent co-operators
with us. They learn to make a proper use of the
freedom of discussion which exists under our government, by observing how we use it ourselves;
and they cease to think of violent remedies, because they are convinced that there is no indis-
position on our part to satisfy every real want of
the country. Dishonest and bad rulers alone de-

rive any advantage from the ignorance of their
subjects. As long as we study the benefit of
India in our measures, the confidence and affection of the people will increase in proportion to
their knowledge of us.

But this is not all. There is a principle in
human nature which impels all mankind to aim at
improving their condition: every individual has
his plan of happiness: every community has its
ideas of securing the national honour and prosperity. This powerful and universal principle, in
some shape or other, is in a state of constant
activity; and if it be not enlisted on our side, it must
be arrayed against us. As long as the natives
are left to brood over their former independence,
their sole specific for improving their condition is,
the immediate and total expulsion of the English.
A native patriot of the old school has no notion of
any thing beyond this : his attention has never
been called to any other mode of restoring the
dignity and prosperity of his country. It is only
by the infusion of European ideas, that a new direction can be given to the national views. The
young men, brought up at our seminaries, turn
with contempt from the barbarous despotisms
under which their ancestors groaned, to the prospect of improving their national institutions on

the English model.   Instead of regarding us with
dislike, they court our society, and look upon us
as their natural protectors and benefactors : the
summit of their ambition is, to resemble us; and,
under our auspices, they hope to elevate the character of their countrymen, and to prepare them
by gradual steps for the enjoyment of a well-
regulated and therefore a secure and a happy
independence.   So far from having the idea of
driving the English into the sea uppermost in
their minds, they have no notion of any improvement but such as rivets their connection with the
English, and makes them dependent on English
protection and instruction.   In the re-establishment of the old native governments they see only
the destruction of their most cherished hopes, and
a state of great personal insecurity for themselves.

The existing connection between two such distant countries as England and India, cannot, in
the nature of things, be permanent: no effort of
policy can prevent the natives from ultimately
regaining their independence.   But there are two
ways of arriving at this point.   One of these is,
through the medium of revolution; the other,
through that of reform.   In one, the forward
movement is sudden and violent; in the other, it
is gradual and peaceable.   One must end in a

complete alienation of mind and separation of interests between ourselves and the natives; the other in a permanent alliance, founded on mutual benefit and good-will.

The only means at our disposal for preventing the one and securing the other class of results is, to set the natives on a process of European improvement, to which they are already sufficiently inclined. They will then cease to desire and aim at independence on the old Indian footing. A sudden change will then be impossible; and a long continuance of our present connection with India will even be assured to us. A Mahratta or Mahommedan despotism might be re-established in a month; but a century would scarcely suffice to prepare the people for self-government on the European model. The political education of a nation must be a work of time; and while it is in progress, we shall be as safe as it will be possible for us to be. The natives will not rise against us, because we shall stoop to raise them: there will be no reaction, because there will be no pressure: the national activity will be fully and harmlessly employed in acquiring and diffusing European knowledge, and in naturalising European institutions. The educated classes, knowing that the elevation of their country on these principles can only be

K

worked out under our protection, will naturally cling to us. They even now do so. There is no class of our subjects to whom we are so thoroughly necessary as those whose opinions have been cast in the English mould: they are spoiled for a purely native regime; they have every thing to fear from the premature establishment of a native government; their education would mark them out for persecution: the feelings of independence, the literary and scientific pursuits, the plans of improvement in which they indulged under our government, must be exchanged for the servility and prostration of mind which characterise an Asiatic court. This class is at present a small minority, but it is continually receiving accessions from the youth who are brought up at the different English seminaries. It will in time become the majority; and it will then be necessary to modify the political institutions to suit the increased intelligence of the people, and their capacity for self-government.

The change will thus be peaceably and gradually effected: there will be no struggle, no mutual exasperation; the natives will have independence, after first learning how to make a good use of it: we shall exchange profitable subjects for still more profitable allies. The present administrative connection benefits families, but a strict commercial union between the first manufacturing and the first producing country in the world, would be a solid foundation of strength and prosperity to our whole nation. If this course be adopted, there will, properly speaking, be no separation. A precarious and temporary relation will almost imperceptibly pass into another far more durable and beneficial. Trained by us to happiness and independence, and endowed with our learning and our political institutions, India will remain the proudest monument of British benevolence; and we shall long continue to reap, in the affectionate attachment of the people, and in a great commercial intercourse with their splendid country,* the fruit of that liberal and enlightened policy which suggested to us this line of conduct.

In following this course we should be trying no new experiment. The Romans at once civilised

* The present trade with India can give no idea of what it is capable of becoming the productive powers of the country are immense: the population of British India alone, without including the native States, is more than three times that of all the rest of the British Empire. By governing well, and promoting to the utmost of our power the growth of wealth, intelligence, and enterprise in its vast population, we shall be able to make India a source of wealth and strength to our nation in time to come, with which nothing in our past history furnishes any parallel.

the nations of Europe, and attached them to their
rule by Romanising them; or, in other words, by
educating them in the Roman literature and arts,
and teaching them to emulate their conquerors instead of opposing them.   Acquisitions made by
superiority in war, were consolidated by superiority in the arts of peace ; and the remembrance of
the original violence was lost in that of the benefits which resulted from it.   The provincials of
Italy, Spain, Africa, and Gaul, having no ambition except to imitate the Romans, and to share
their privileges with them, remained to the last
faithful subjects of the empire; and the union was
at last dissolved, not by internal revolt, but by the
shock of external violence, which involved conquerors and conquered in one common overthrow.
The Indians will, I hope, soon stand in the same
position towards us in which we once stood towards
the Romans.   Tacitus informs us, that it was the
policy of Julius Agricola to instruct the sons of
the leading men among the Britons in the literature and science of Rome, and to give them a taste
for the refinements of Roman civilisation.*   We

* The words of Tacitus are, " Jam vero principum filios libera-
libus artibus erudire, et ingenia Britannorum studiis Gallorum an-
teferre, ut qui modo linguam Romanam abnuebant, eloquentiam
concupiscerent.   Inde etiam habitus nostri honor et frequens toga.
Paulatimque discessum ad delinimenta vitiorum, porticus et bal-

all know how well this plan answered. From being obstinate enemies, the Britons soon became attached and confiding friends; and they made more strenuous efforts to retain the Romans, than their ancestors had done to resist their invasion. It will be a shame to us if, with our greatly superior advantages, we also do not make our premature departure be dreaded as a calamity. It must not be said in after ages, that " the groans of the Britons" were elicited by the breaking up of the Roman empire; and the groans of the Indians by the continued existence of the British.

We may also take a lesson from the Mahommetans, whose conquests have been so extensive and so permanent. From the Indian Archipelago to Portugal, Arabic was established as the language of religion, of literature, and of law; the vernacular tongues were saturated with it; and the youth of the conquered countries soon began to vie with their first instructors in every branch of Mahommedan learning. A polite education was understood to mean a Mahommedan education; and the most cultivated and active minds were every where engaged on the side of the Mahommedan system.

---

nea et conviviorum elegantiam ; idque apud imperitos humanitas vocabatur cum pars servitutis esset."

The Emperor Akbar followed up this policy in India. Arabicised Persian was adopted as the language of his dynasty; and the direction thereby given to the national sympathies and ideas greatly contributed to produce that feeling of veneration for the family which has long survived the loss of its power. This feeling, which in Europe would be called loyalty, is common to those who have been brought up in the old learning, but is very rarely found in connection with an English education. The policy of our predecessors, although seldom worthy of imitation, was both very sound and very successful in this respect. If we adopt the same policy, it will be more beneficial to the natives in proportion as English contains a greater fund of true knowledge than Arabic and Persian: and it will be more beneficial to us in proportion as the natives will study English more zealously and extensively than they did Arabic and Persian, and will be more completely changed by it in feeling and opinion.

These views were not worked out by reflection, but were forced on me by actual observation and experience. I passed some years in parts of India, where, owing to the comparative novelty of our rule and to the absence of any attempt to alter the current of native feeling, the national habits of

thinking remained unchanged. There, high and
low, rich and poor, had only one idea of improving
their political condition. The upper classes lived
upon the prospect of regaining their former pre-
eminence; and the lower, upon that of having the
avenues to wealth and distinction re-opened to them
by the re-establishment of a native government.
Even sensible and comparatively well affected natives had no notion that there was any remedy for
the existing depressed state of their nation except
the sudden and absolute expulsion of the English.
After that, I resided for some years in Bengal, and
there I found quite another set of ideas prevalent
among the educated natives. Instead of thinking
of cutting the throats of the English, they were
aspiring to sit with them on the grand jury or on
the bench of magistrates. Instead of speculating
on Punjab or Nepaulese politics, they were dis-
cussing the advantages of printing and free discussion, in oratorical English speeches, at debating
societies which they had established among themselves. The most sanguine dimly looked forward
in the distant future to the establishment of a
national representative assembly as the consum-
mation of their hopes—all of them being fully
sensible that these plans of improvement could
only be worked out with the aid and protection of

the British Government by the gradual improvement of their countrymen in knowledge and
morality; and that the re-establishment of a Mahommedan or any other native regime would at once
render all such views impracticable and ridiculous.
No doubt, both these schemes of national improvement suppose the termination of the English
rule: but while that event is the beginning of
one, it is only the conclusion of the other.   In one,
the sudden and violent overthrow of our government is a necessary preliminary : in the other, a
long continuance of our administration, and the
gradual withdrawal of it as the people become fit
to govern themselves, are equally indispensable.

Our native army is justly regarded as the pillar
of our Indian empire; and no plan of benefiting
either the natives or ourselves can be worth anything which does not rest on the supposition that
this pillar will remain unbroken.   It is therefore
of importance to inquire how this essential element of power is likely to be affected by the
course of policy which has been described.   The
Indian army is made up of two· entirely distinct
parts; the English officers, and the native officers
and men.   The former will, under any circumstances, stand firm to their national interests:
the latter will be animated by the feelings of the

class of society from which they are drawn, except so far as those feelings may be modified by professional interests and habits. The native officers rise from the ranks; and the ranks are recruited from the labouring class, which is the last that will be affected by any system of national education. Not one in five hundred of the boys who are instructed in the Zillah seminaries, will enlist in the army. If the Sepoys are educated anywhere, it must be in the village schools; and the organisation of those schools will be the concluding measure of the series. The instruction given to the labouring class can never be more than merely elementary. They have not leisure for more. But, such as it is, they will be indebted for it to us; and as it will form part of a system established and superintended by ourselves, we shall take care that it is of a kind calculated to inspire feelings of attachment to the British connection. After this, the young men who enlist in the army will become imbued with the military spirit, and moulded by the habits of military obedience. I leave to others to judge whether this training is calculated to make better and more attached, or worse and more disaffected, soldiers than the state of entire neglect, as regards their moral and intellectual improvement, in which the whole class.

are at present left. I never heard that the education given in the national schools unfitted the common people of England for the ranks of the army; although the inducements to honourable and faithful service, which are open to them after they enter the army, are much inferior to those which are held out to our Sepoys.

Religious instruction forms no part of the object of the Government seminaries. It would be impossible for the State to interfere at all with native education on any other condition; and this is now so well understood, that religious jealousy offers no obstruction to our success. The general favour with which English education is regarded, and the multitudes who flock to our schools, prove this to be the case. The Brahmins, it is true, ruled supreme over the old system. It was moulded for the express purpose of enabling them to hold the minds of men in thraldom; and ages had fixed the stamp of solidity upon it. Upon this ground they were unassailable. But popular education, through the medium of the English language, is an entirely new element, with which they are incapable of dealing. It did not enter into the calculation of the founders of their system; and they have no machinery to oppose to it. Although they have been priest-ridden for ages, the people of India are, for all purposes of improvement, a new, and more than a new, people. Their appetite for knowledge has been whetted by their long-compelled fast; and aware of the superiority of the new learning, they devour it more greedily than they ever would have done Sanskrit lore, even if that lore had not been withheld from them: they bring to the task, vacant minds and excited curiosity, absence of prejudice, and an inextinguishable thirst for information. They cannot return under the dominion of the Brahmins. The spell has been for ever broken. Hinduism is not a religion which will bear examination. It is so entirely destitute of any thing like evidence, and is identified with so many gross immoralities and physical absurdities, that it gives way at once before the light of European science. Mahommedanism is made of tougher materials; yet, even a Mahommedan youth who has received an English education is a very different person from one who has been taught according to the perfect manner of the law of his fathers. As this change advances, India will become quite another country: nothing more will be heard of excitable religious feelings: priestcraft will no longer be able to work by ignorance: knowledge and power will pass from a dominant caste to the people themselves; the whole nation will co-operate with us in reforming institutions, the possibility of altering which could never have been contemplated if events had taken any other course; and many causes will concur to introduce a more wholesome state of morals, which, of all the changes that can take place, is the one in which the public welfare is most concerned.

There has been a time at which each of the other branches of the public service has particularly commanded attention. The commercial, the political, the judicial, the revenue departments, have in turn been the subject of special consideration; and decisive steps have been taken to put them on a satisfactory footing. My object will be sufficiently attained if I succeed in producing a conviction that the time has arrived for taking up the question of public instruction in the same spirit, and with the same determination to employ whatever means may be requisite for accomplishing the object in view. The absence of any sensible proof that increased taxation is attended with any proportionate benefit to India, has long been extremely disheartening both to the natives and to the European public officers serving in that country.* The entire abolition of the transit duties,

* A large proportion of the land in the Bengal and Agra Presidencies is held tax-free; but, although nothing can be more

and the establishment of an adequate system of
public instruction, would furnish this proof, and
would excite the warmest gratitude of every body
who from any cause feels interested in the welfare
of India. The interest of a single million sterling *,
in addition to what is already expended, would be
sufficient to answer every present purpose as far
as education is concerned. Even on the narrow-
est view of national interest, a million could not
be better invested. It would ensure the moral and
intellectual emancipation of the people of India,
and would render them at once attached to our
rule and worthy of our alliance.

---

unreasonable than that persons who benefit by the protection of
the Government should contribute nothing to its support, and
throw the whole burden on the rest, it is impossible at present to
induce the natives to view the subject in this light. Their in-
variable answer is, that while it is certain that some will be worse
off, they see no reason to suppose that they will themselves be
better off if the exempted lands are brought under contribution.

* The Parliamentary assignment of ten thousand pounds a
year still remains to be accounted for to the Committee of
public instruction, from July 1813 to May 1821, with compound
interest up to the date of payment.

APPENDIX.

Extract from the Report of the Committee appointed by the Indian Government to inquire into the State of Medical Education.

AGREEABLY to your Lordship's direction to that effect, we called upon Mr. Tytler to prepare a synopsis of what he conceives the pupils at the Institution should be taught in the different branches of medical science. This document, according to our view of it, does not contain by any means such a comprehensive and improved scheme of education as the circumstances of the case indicate the absolute necessity of. Leaving it entirely out of the question, then, at present, we would very respectfully submit to your Lordship in council our serious opinion, that the best mode of fulfilling the great ends under consideration, is for the state to found a Medical College for the education of natives ; in which the various branches of medical science cultivated in Europe should be taught, and as near as possible on the most approved European system ; the basis of which system should be a reading and writing knowledge on the part of candidate pupils of the English language, and the like knowledge of Hindustanee or Bengallee, and a knowledge of arithmetic ; inclusive, of course, of proper qualifications as to health, age, and respectability of conduct. The Government might select from the various young men, who should pass the final examination, the most distinguished and deserving, for filling up va-

cancies as sub-assistant surgeons. A knowledge of the Eng
lish language, we consider as a *sine qua non*, because that
language combines within itself the circle of all the sciences
and incalculable wealth of printed works and illustrations,
circumstances that give it obvious advantages over the oriental languages, in which are only to be found the crudest
elements of science, or the most irrational substitutes for it.

Of the perfect feasibility of such a proposal, we do not
entertain a doubt : nevertheless, like any other, it will be
found to divide the opinions of men of talent and experience.
These will divide into an Oriental and an English party.
Mr. Tytler's long replies have imposed upon us the necessity of entering at greater length into the argument respecting the feasibility of the contemplated plan, than we could
have wished. We beg to apologise to your Lordship for
this circumstance, but as Mr, Tytler, instead of giving brief
and simple answers to our questions, preferred committing
them to paper in the form of long minutes ; it became incumbent upon us to offer something in the way of refutation.
The determined Orientalist having himself acquired the
Sanscrit and the Arabic, at the cost of much and severe application, as well as of pecuniary expense, will view with
great repugnance a suggestion of teaching science in such a
way as may cast his peculiar pursuits into the shade, and independent of a language which he reveres as classical. The
advocate for the substitution of the English language, on
the other hand, will doubt whether the whole stores of
Eastern literature have enabled us to ascertain a single fact
of the least consequence towards the history of the ancient
world ; whether they have tended to improve morality, or
to extend science ; or whether, with the exception of what
the Arabian physicians derived from the Greeks, the Arabic
contains a sufficient body of scientific information to reward
the modern medical student for all the labour and attention
that would be much more profitably bestowed on the study

of the English language ; and lastly, whether the modicum of unscientific medical literature contained in the Sanscrit is worth undergoing the enormous trouble of acquiring that language

Unlike the languages of Europe, which are keys to vast intellectual treasures, bountifully to reward the literary inquirer, those of the East, save to a limited extent in poetry and romance, may be said, without exaggeration, to be next to barren. For history and science, then, and all that essentially refines and adorns, we must not look to Oriental writers.

Mr. Tytler has favoured us with his opinions, on the question under consideration, at great length. The Rev. Mr. Duff, whose experience in instructing native youth is extensive and valuable, has also obliged us with his sentiments on the subject; which are entirely at issue with those of Mr. Tytler, who takes up the Oriental side of the question with equal ardour and ingenuity.

Mr. Tytler denies that a system of educating the natives through the medium of English would be in the least more comprehensive, or by any means so much so, as one carried on in the native languages (Mr. Tytler, in that phrase including Sanscrit, Arabic, and Persian) ; and considers it wholly inexpedient as a general measure.

The Rev. Mr. Duff, on the other hand, although acknowledging that the native languages, by which we understand the Bengallee in the lower provinces, and the Oordoo in the higher, alone are available for imparting an elementary education to the mass of the people, affirms that the popular language does not afford an adequate medium for communicating a knowledge of the higher departments of literature and science, &c. " No original works of the description wanted," he observes, " have yet appeared in the native languages ; and though much of a highly useful nature has been provided through European talent and perseverance no translations have been made in any degree sufficient to supply materials for the prosecution of the higher object contemplated; neither is it likely, in the nature of things, that either by original publications, or translations of standard works, the deficiency can be fully or adequately remedied, for such a number of years to come, as may leave the whole of the present generation sleeping with their fathers." (Answer to Question 20, p. 17.)

Mr. Tytler's reasons for his unfavourable opinion, in regard to the proposed plan, arise, he informs us, partly from the nature of language in general, and partly from the intrinsic difficulty of English itself. The difficulty, it strikes us, is magnified in Mr. Tytler's imagination, and at any rate can scarcely be greater than that of acquiring Arabic and Sanscrit, which are about as foreign to the body of the people as English. " A bare knowledge of the English," observes Mr. Tytler, " or of the words for objects, is plainly no increase of knowledge, unless it be accompanied with some additional information respecting the objects of which the words are the signs." This is so self-evident a truism, that we are rather surprised Mr. Tytler should deem the stating of it of any use to his argument. The mere capability of uttering the word *opium*, for instance, would be of little use, unless accompanied by a knowledge of the qualities of that drug. It is not with a view to recommend a knowledge of mere words that we troubled Mr. Tytler for his opinion, and have now the honour of addressing your Lordship; but to rescue, if possible, the course of native medical education from this its pervading and crying evil ; for assuredly, nothing, that has yet been made manifest to us tends to show that the pupils of the Institution, under the present system, acquire much beyond mere words; or to demonstrate, that an acquaintance with Sanscrit and Arabic vocables will give better ideas of things important to be known than English. In fact, to teach English science, English words must be used; or, in their stead, Arabic and Sanscrit ones must be coined. With the highest opinion of Mr. Tytler's talents, acquirements, and zeal, and the greatest respect for his character, yet must we not be blinded to a certain degree of partisanship, which unconsciously, we doubt not, has apparently warped his otherwise excellent judgment on this question. A discrepancy in his opinions on this subject, however, appears to exist; for he would, to a certain extent, teach the pupils on English principles. If your Lordship will turn to Mr. Tytler's synopsis, it will there be seen, that he proposes to teach the pupils the Latin and English names of the corporeal organs, and of the articles of the materia medica. For this purpose he would instruct them in the English system of spelling and pronunciation, in the declension of Latin nouns, and their rules of concordance. He would, in a word, lead them to the half-way house of English education, and there stop.

"English" proceeds Mr. Tytler, "is one of the most difficult of all languages, and the most diversified in its origin. It arises from three sources — Saxon, Latin, and Norman-French, Its words and idioms vary in accordance with these three. Hence, a correct knowledge of it can be obtained only by a certain degree of knowledge of all the originals." For the attainment of a hypercritical or highly scholastic knowledge, such as is not possessed by one Englishman out of a hundred, Mr. Tytler's position may be readily acceded to. How many thousands are there, however, of Englishmen, persons of ability and intelligence in various walks of active usefulness, who know nothing, or next to nothing, of pure Saxon, Latin, and Norman-French? Nay, there is reason to suppose that there are not a few skilful and experienced surgeons not better versed in these languages, but who are valuable men in the profession notwithstanding. Will a native sub-assistant surgeon be the less capable of being taught to amputate a limb, because he can-

not give the critical etymology of the words *knife, limb, cut ?*
Surely the great ends of life are not to stand still for want of
knowledge of scholastic roots ? It would be superfluous to
point out, in a more elaborate manner, how very overstrained,
and inapplicable to general experience, Mr. Tytler's argument is.

As very apposite to the subject under consideration, we
beg to submit an extract or two from a forcible article by
the late Dr. Duncan, jun., on Medical Education, which was
published in the Edinburgh Medical and Surgical Journal
for 1827. " The knowledge of languages, in itself, derives
its chief utility from its facilitating the acquisition of useful
knowledge ; and, therefore, as the mind may be nearly
equally disciplined during the acquisition of any one language
as of any other, their utility is directly proportional to the
value of the information contained in the books written in
them." Tried by this test, how utterly mispent must be the
time devoted by the native medical student to the study of
Arabic, Sanscrit, and Persian ! " It is argued," continues
the article quoted, " in favour of the study of the Greek
language, that it is the language of the fathers of physic ;
and that the terms of medical art have been almost all
borrowed from it and the Latin ; and that it seems impossible to understand properly their meaning, without possessing
some knowledge of the sources from which they have been
derived." The first argument would be nearly equally conclusive in favour of the Arabic, that physicians might read Avicenna and Rhazes in the original ; and with regard to the last,
we shall reply, on the authority of Dugald Stewart. " It is in
many cases a fortunate circumstance when the words we
employ have lost their pedigree, or (what amounts nearly to
the same thing,) when it can be traced by those alone who
are skilled in ancient and modern languages. Such words
have in their favour the sanction of immemorial usage, and

the obscurity of their history prevents them from misleading the imagination, by recalling to it the objects or phenomena to which they owed their origin. The notions, accordingly, we annex to them, may be expected to be peculiarly precise and definite." (Stewart's Phil. Essay, p. 184.) Indeed all attempts at descriptive terminology have utterly failed, and have impeded, instead of advancing, the progress of knowledge. " Medicine (observes the same eminent writer, in another place,) is a practical profession. That knowledge is most essential to its students, which renders them the most useful servants of the public ; and all reputation for extrinsic learning (such, for instance, as Sanscrit and Arabic,) which is acquired at the expense of practical skill, is meretricious, and deceives the public, by dazzling their judgment."

Although Mr. Tytler has throughout, unconsciously to himself, we doubt not, overstrained his argument, yet is there one passage which, we are free to confess, trenches on the extravagant. " The great sources of our language," he states, " must be shown; the Saxon, the Latin, and the French. We must explain what words and what idioms are derived from each, and what changes they have undergone in their passage. Till this be all done, difficult as it may seem, we may by much practice impress upon the natives a sort of jargon, and agree to call it English ; but it will bear scarcely more resemblance to real English than to the dialect of the Hottentots." In a word, if we do not make lexicographers of native sub-assistant surgeons, they will not be able to set a fracture, or to prescribe a dose of calomel ; and their English remarks or directions, though perfectly intelligible, will amount, in fact, to nothing but a Hottentot jargon ! Need we, in refutation of this exaggerated view, remind your Lordship, that there are many respectable native gentlemen in Calcutta, who both speak and write English correctly and fluently ? The works of the late Rammohan Roy were not

written in a Hottentot dialect; and at this moment there are
three newspapers in Calcutta printed in the English language,
and yet edited by natives. Why should not other native students be equally successful with those alluded to? We
readily grant that much is to be yet done to render the English language more popular in India; but assuredly the most
likely way of effecting this very desirable end, is not to bestow a premium upon the study of the Arabic, Sanscrit, and
Persian, and to close the portal of employment to the English student.

According to Mr. Tytler, it is not only the difficulty of
acquiring the English, which is such a formidable obstacle in
the way of the learner, but the almost insurmountable one of
finding properly qualified English teachers. We beg to refer
your lordship to his observations on this head, contenting
ourselves with the remark, that if English is not to be taught
to native medical students, until such an utopian selection of
schoolmasters as Mr. Tytler indicates be made, then must
the English language, and the treasures of scientific knowledge it contains, be long to them a fountain sealed.

Mr. Tytler has several elaborate comments on the study
of Greek and Latin, the scope of which is to show, that these
languages have a greater affinity to the English language, than
English has to Sanscrit, Arabic, and Persian. The argument
is ingenious, but far from conclusive. Latin and Greek, indeed, were the languages of the learned in Europe, as Arabic and Sanscrit are of the learned in India. There the
parallel ends. English, however, enjoys an advantage that
Latin did not at the epoch alluded to by Mr. Tytler. It
is a living language; it is the language of a great people,
many of whom, it may now be expected, will settle in this
country; it is also the language of the governing power. It
is not too much to expect that the time is not far distant
when English will become much more popular than it is, and

when to speak and write it correctly will be deemed a distinguishing privilege. Let English have fair play, and be placed at least upon a par with Sancrit, Arabic, and Persian, and it will become manifest to the most indifferent observer, that the natives study the latter, not because they are the best media for instruction, but because they lead to employment and competency, which the English does not. Perhaps an exception should be stated with reference to the Sanscrit— judging from a recent memorial of a number of Hindu youths to the secretary of the sub-committee to the Sanscrit College, representing, that after many years spent in the study of Sancrit, they are in a destitute condition, as they can find neither employment nor consideration among their countrymen.

So long as European literature was confined to Latin, Mr. Tytler estimates the attempts of our ancestors as mere forced imitations of the classics, the far greater part of which are now deservedly forgotten. Supposing the fact to be even as stated, it cuts both ways ; and we may, by a parity of reasoning, assume, that so long as Eastern literature is confined to Sanscrit, Arabic, and Persian, the writings of Indian students will be mere forced imitations of the Sanscrit, Arabic, and Persian classics. But Mr. Tytler is a great deal too sweeping in his remarks; for many of the works of our ancestors in science, morals, and poetry, that were written in Latin, so far from being forgotten, are held in the highest estimation, even at this day, and are remarkable no less for strength of reasoning than for purity and elegance of expression. We shall be perfectly content if native students should be found to think as justly, and write as beautifully, in English, as Buchanan, Bacon, and various others did in Latin ; or, to come nearer our own times, and in a professional walk, as Harvey, Sydenham, Boerhaave, Haller, Heberden, and Gregory did, in the same language.

It should be borne in mind, that when Latin was, it may be said, the cradle of science, the English language had not attained that fulness and correctness of which it can now legitimately boast. The style of vernacular writers was not formed, being quaint, pedantic, and vitiated; composition was in its infancy, and there were but few writers. The times, too, were far from favourable to the cultivation of letters.

To compare English composition as it was in those days, with what it afterwards became, would be to institute a comparison between a Hindoo figure-maker and Canova. Ever since the Reformation, the English language has been advancing to its present magnificent state of universality, copiousness, and beauty. It would, indeed, be a strange thing, if in our day, when more works are published in a year than were in the olden time printed in half a century, the native youth of India, who may turn to the study of English, should, in defiance of the standard works put into their hands, and in spite of precept and example, follow such pedantic and vitiated models as those alluded to by Mr. Tytler. Facts daily occurring around us, demonstrate the groundlessness of such a fear.

" As it was in Europe," contends Mr. Tytler, " so it will be with the English productions of the natives of India; they will be a mere patchwork of sentences extracted from the few English books with which their authors are acquainted." Mr. Tytler should at least have shown, that, to produce such an effect, the circumstances were precisely the same in the two countries. How he has reached his postulate, he has not condescended to say ; nor is it of much importance to know ; for it is, after all, a hypothetical assumption. In recommending that native medical students should possess a knowledge of English, we are swayed by a hope, not of their writing books, good or bad, but of their thoroughly understanding and digesting valuable works in that language, comprising as it does an inestimable body of scientific information; and in progress of time, of their translating them into the vernacular tongues of India, for the benefit of their countrymen. We wish them to be able to drink at the fountain-head, instead of depending to allay their mental thirst with driblets of translations, occasionally from the hands of an European.

But the exclusive study of English, Mr. Tytler deems, will be chargeable with producing an effect which he greatly deprecates. It must necessarily, he thinks, discourage the natives from the cultivation of their own tongues. Were Arabic and Persian their own tongues, there would be some show of reason in the objection ; but when we bear in mind that they are as foreign to the people as English, its validity vanishes at once. To the great body of the people, too, the Sanscrit is in effect quite a foreign language.. Of the absorption of that language we need have no fear, so long as it is the interest of the Brahmins to foster it. But if the thing were possible, we are by no means disposed to view the substitution of English for these tongues as a misfortune. As to the objection, that the study of English would put an end to all native composition and indigenous literature ; we would simply inquire, if there is in the world a less edifying and more barren literature than that of Hindoostan, or one that has done less for morality, philosophy, and science ?

With reference to that imitation of English writers, which Mr. Tytler assumes would beset native students, that gentleman quotes with complacency a saying of Johnson, " That no man was ever great by imitation," and amplifies the apophthegm so as to comprehend masses of men ; as if the saying stood, that no people ever became great by imitation. The saying thus applied, becomes an untenable sophism ; for, on reflection, we shall find that the converse of the position holds true; since civilisation itself is nothing else but a complex system of imitation.

L

We beg now to call your Lordship's attention to the opinions of the Rev. Mr. Duff. In reply to the question, whether, in order to teach the principles of any science to native boys, he considered it necessary that they should know Sanscrit, Arabic, and Persian ? the reverend gentleman replies, that, " In reference to the acquisition of European science, the study of the languages mentioned would be a sheer waste of labour and time ; since, viewed as a media for receiving and treasuring the stores of modern science, there is, at present, no possible connection between them." On the other hand, in reply to the question,— if he thought it possible to teach native boys the principles of any science through the medium of the English language ? He replied, that, " The experience of the last three years has, if possible, confirmed the conviction he previously entertained, not merely that it is possible to teach native boys the principles of any science through the medium of the English language, but that, in the present incipient state of native improvement, it is next to impossible to teach them successfully the principles of any science through any other medium than the English." He further records his opinion, that the study of the English language might be rendered very popular among the natives. " The sole reason," he justly observes, " why the English is not now more a general and anxious object of acquisition among the natives, is the degree of uncertainty under which they (the natives) still labour as to the ultimate intentions of Government, and whether it will ever lead them into paths of usefulness, profit, or honour; only let the intentions of Government be officially announced, and there will be a general movement among all the more respectable classes." But the teaching of English acquires much importance, when we consider it, with Mr. Duff, as the grand remedy for obviating the prejudices of the natives against practical anatomy. " The English language," he urges (Mr. Duff's replies, p. 32.), " opens up a whole world of new ideas, and examples of success in every department of science; and the ideas so true, and the examples so striking, work mightily on the susceptible minds of native youth; so that by the time they have acquired a mastery over the English language, under judicious and enlightened instructors, their minds are almost metamorphosed into the texture and cast of European youth, and they cannot help expressing their utter contempt for Hindoo superstition and prejudices."

There is an argument of fact put in by Mr. Duff, which is admirably to the point. We allude to the introduction of the English language and of English science among the Scottish Highlanders, whose native language, to this day, is the Gaelic. The parallel is a very fair one; for no people were more superstitious, more wedded to their own customs, and more averse to leaving their native country, than the Highlanders: but since the introduction of the English language among them, the state of things is much changed. The same observation applies to Ireland and Wales, where, as in the Highlands of Scotland, the English is a foreign language; and yet its acquisition is eagerly sought after by the natives of all these countries, as an almost certain passport to employment. There are medical men, natives of these countries, scattered all over the world, whose mother tongue is Welsh, Irish, or Gaelic, which, as children, they spoke for years—just as the children of European parents in India speak Hindoostanee and Bengalee; with this difference, however, that the latter soon forget the Oriental tongues; while the youth who acquire the indigenous language of Ireland, the Scottish Highlands, and Wales, never lose the language of those countries, because they do not quit them till a more advanced period of life. For the first years of youth the Highlanders at school, even of all ranks, think in the Gaelic; but this does not prevent their acquiring such a fluent and business-like knowledge of English, as to enable them to pass through life with credit, and not unfrequently with distinction. What is there in the condition, physical or moral, of the natives of this country, that should render them incapable of acquiring English as easily as the Irish, the Highlanders, and Welsh?

(Signed)   J. GRANT, - - - - President.

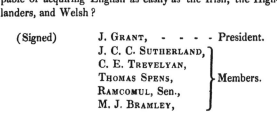

J. C. C. SUTHERLAND,
C. E. TREVELYAN,
THOMAS SPENS,   } Members.
RAMCOMUL, Sen.,
M. J. BRAMLEY,

THE END.

LONDON;
Printed by A. SPOTTISWOODE,
New-Street-Square.

For EU product safety concerns, contact us at Calle de José Abascal, 56–1°, 28003 Madrid, Spain or eugpsr@cambridge.org.